Essays in Honor of
ANSCAR J. CHUPUNGCO, O.S.B.

Wilton D. Gregory

John R. Page

Gilbert Ostdiek, O.F.M.

Burkhard Neunheuser, O.S.B.

Keith F. Pecklers, S.J.

Mark R. Francis, C.S.V.

Margaret Mary Kelleher, O.S.U.

Dominic E. Serra

Michael G. Witczak

Gordon W. Lathrop

Bernardo Ma. Pérez, O.S.B.

Cassian Folsom, O.S.B.

Editors

Mark R. Francis, C.S.V., and Keith F. Pecklers, S.J.

Liturgy for the New Millennium

*A Commentary on
the Revised Sacramentary*

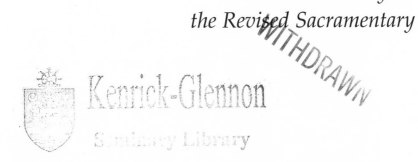
Essays in Honor
of Anscar J. Chupungco, O.S.B.

A PUEBLO BOOK

The Liturgical Press Collegeville, Minnesota

A Pueblo Book published by The Liturgical Press

Design by Frank Kacmarcik, Obl.S.B.

Library of Congress Cataloging-in-Publication Data

Francis, Mark R.
    Liturgy for the new millennium : a commentary on the revised Sacramentary : essays in honor of Anscar J. Chupungco / Mark R. Francis, Keith F. Pecklers ; editors, Wilton D. Gregory . . . [et al.].
    p. cm.
    "A Pueblo book".
    Includes bibliographical references.
    ISBN 0-8146-6174-2 (alk. paper)
    1. Catholic Church.   Sacramentary (U.S.)   I. Chupungco, Anscar J. II. Pecklers, Keith F., 1958– .   III. Gregory, Wilton D. IV. Title.
BX2037.A4F73   2000
264'.02036—dc21
                                      99-27733
                                      CIP

Contents

Foreword

"It is enough for the disciple that he become like the teacher."
(Matthew 10:25)

As I compose this Foreword for the *Festschrift* in honor of the sixtieth birthday observance of Anscar J. Chupungco, O.S.B., I am drawn to this particular scriptural citation as an appropriate expression of my personal esteem and respect for Professor Chupungco. I know that I also write this tribute on behalf of all of those who will open this work with similar memories of working with Anscar as his students.

I am privileged to claim the honor of being Anscar's first doctoral candidate—a title that is entirely the dignity of a chronological coincidence. Anscar's scholarship and his professional expertise in ways far more profound than my initial experience of his tutelage no doubt have influenced and continue to influence dozens of other students of liturgy.

Working with Anscar in doctoral studies was a marvelous exercise in being introduced to critical thinking, to careful research, and to intellectual character-building which he always both demonstrated and expected in return. Anscar never allowed his opinions to overpower the thoughts of this neophyte scholar. However, he demanded that judicious study, respected sources, and reputable authorities always buttress the opinions of his students. He invited us to build upon a solid knowledge of the liturgical tradition of the Church. However, this invitation was always to allow a reverence for the past to prepare for the liturgical future of the Church. Such was his contribution to my own liturgical education and many others as well, I am sure.

Anscar's own personal history was an obvious preparation for his important contribution to the world of liturgical studies. As a Benedictine monk of Our Lady of Montserrat Abbey in Manila and himself a student of Burkhard Neunheuser from Maria Laach, Adrian Nocent (d. 1996) from Maredsous, Jordi Pinell (d. 1997) from

Montserrat, and Salvatore Marsili (d. 1983) from Finalpia—to mention only a few of his own professors—he is a living link to the classic liturgical heritage of Europe.

He found in the scholarship of many of those who were pioneer thinkers preparing for the momentous work of the liturgical reforms that resulted from the Second Vatican Council, the impetus for his own works.

As a son of a culture born from Western and Eastern parentage, Anscar always recognized the importance of inculturation. Indeed, he witnessed it in the amalgam of cultures that thrive in the Philippines. His heritage and his studies made it both reasonable and appropriate that he turn his scholarly attention to the matters of inculturation as a vital contemporary expression of a long and rich liturgical heritage.

His interests in this area of liturgical scholarship and his related pastoral suggestions have not always received a sympathetic hearing. He has dared to challenge the Church to respond to the conditions and aspirations of people whose cultural heritages are not represented in Western civilization. At the same time, he has urged the Church to reflect upon its own long and rich heritage of accepting contributions from the nascent cultures that were once establishing the foundations of what is now the venerable and well-established Western civilization.

The closing decades of the second millennium of Christianity find the Church facing many similar challenges to those that it faced at the beginning of the first Christian millennium. The Church is home to many people whose background is foreign to that of established Catholicism. In addition, even people who are quite Western in thought and circumstances are asking for special considerations and indulgences when engaging in the worship of the Church. People who are not unique because of language, ethnic, or racial differences, but because of age, gender, or ideological preferences have claimed for themselves the term "culture." Must the Church accept all of these various differences and respond to them as indeed separate cultures? Will not such fragmentation only lead to further disunity rather than Oneness in Christ? These are not easy questions for anyone whose scholarship and life's work include liturgy.

The paradigms that once worked quite well in reviewing the issue of inculturation simply may no longer apply in this postmodern environment. Anscar's academic approach has always been to return to

Introduction

Anscar Chupungco, O.S.B., has been one of the most important figures in the international postconciliar reform of the liturgy because of
the special vision he brings to liturgical renewal. Best known for his
work on liturgical inculturation, his influence has also extended
throughout the world as a consultor to the Congregation for Divine
Worship in Rome and the International Commission on English in
the Liturgy (ICEL). His leadership of the Pontifical Liturgical Institute
(PIL) in Rome and his founding of the Paul VI Liturgical Institute in
the Philippines for advancing liturgical renewal in Asia witnesses to
an international vision that sees farther afield than either Rome or his
native land. That his vision ranges farther than the confines of the
Roman Catholic Church is illustrated by Anscar's close collaboration
with the Lutheran World Federation and their study of liturgical inculturation at their ecumenical consultations in Switzerland, Hong
Kong, Kenya, and the United States.

In many ways, Anscar's international and culturally sensitive vision has contributed greatly to the work of revising the 1970 translation of the *editio typica* of the *Ordo Missae*. Colleagues in this endeavor
now fittingly offer these essays honoring a collaborator and friend by
treating various aspects of the current revision of the sacramentary.
In the Foreword, Bishop Wilton Gregory, Anscar's first doctoral student at the Pontifical Liturgical Institute, sets the tone for the rest of
the contributions to this volume by noting that the scholarship that
Anscar encouraged has always nurtured a reverence for the liturgical
tradition of the Church as the only sure basis in proposing new possibilities for the worship of the future.

The first essay of this volume by John Page, executive secretary of
ICEL, traces the history and process of the Sacramentary revision
which has involved a wide consultation with the English-speaking

conferences of bishops around the world, assisted by scores of experts in the fields of liturgy, theology, literature, anthropology, and pastoral care. Gilbert Ostdiek presents an inside look into the fascinating but demanding field of liturgical translation, demonstrating that the success of a translated liturgical text involves much more than a literal rendering of the Latin texts, but a real concern for the genius of the English language and a respect for the assembly at prayer. Fr. Burkhard Neunheuser, O.S.B., Anscar's doctoral mentor and his predecessor as president of the PIL, examines the cultural foundation for the present Order of Mass by looking at the nature of the "Genius of the Roman Rite" as seen through the lens of the British liturgical historian Edmund Bishop.

Keith Pecklers studies the role of the liturgical assembly throughout the Church's history and discusses pastoral issues facing the liturgical assembly today in light of current sociological research. One of the most liturgically problematic aspects of the 1969 Rite of Mass was the Entrance Rites. Mark Francis considers the various new options for beginning Mass proposed in the revised Sacramentary. Margaret Mary Kelleher gives us a look at the mandate, rationale, and process by which new prayer texts have been proposed for the revised Sacramentary. The pastoral option of restoring the greeting of peace to its ancient location at the conclusion of the Liturgy of the Word is critiqued by Dominic Serra, who offers both the history and theology of this gesture in the Rite of Mass. Michael Witczak begins his essay with an overview of current research on the subject of Eucharistic Prayers. He then provides a comparative look at the old and new translations of these prayers as well as several new compositions. Gordon Lathrop, well-known Lutheran liturgical theologian, both affirms and challenges this latest fruit of the liturgical reform of the Roman Catholic Church. Locating the discussion in a broader ecumenical context, he examines the role that the revised Sacramentary can play in the liturgical renewal of other churches.

Bernardo Pérez, a fellow Benedictine and Anscar's lifelong friend, gives us an insight into Chupungco's personal and professional history as seen from the perspective of the Philippines and his home monastery, Our Lady of Monserrat in Manila. Current president of the Pontifical Liturgical Institute, Cassian Folsom records the breadth and scope of Anscar's contribution to that institution over the years as professor, president of the Institute, and rector of the Athenaeum of Sant' Anselmo.

xiv

We would like to express our deep gratitude to Michael Naughton, O.S.B., for his support and willingness to publish this commentary on the revised Sacramentary. Thanks go to Daniel J. Merz, doctoral student in liturgy at the PIL, who compiled Anscar's bibliography, and to Christian Göbel assisted by Oswald McBride, O.S.B., for translating the article by Burkhard Neunheuser.

Having been directed in our doctoral work by Anscar Chupungco, we are in his debt. This volume is a token of our appreciation for Anscar's ministry to the liturgical life of the universal and local church and we dedicate it to him with the hope that it will serve the ongoing implementation of the liturgical vision of Vatican II. This vision, so well lived by Anscar, helps us to see God's Spirit in a living and dynamic tradition of people at worship who will continue to give God praise into the new millennium.

Mark R. Francis, C.S.V.
Keith F. Pecklers, S.J.
June 29, 1999
Feast of Saints Peter and Paul

John R. Page

The Process of Revision of the Sacramentary, 1981–98

> Direct our actions, Lord, by your holy inspiration
> and carry them forward by your gracious help,
> that all our works may begin in you
> and by you be happily ended.
>
> We ask this through our Lord Jesus Christ, your Son,
>   who lives and reigns with you in the unity of the Holy Spirit,
> God for ever and ever.
>
> * * *

Historians, at least of an old-fashioned variety, like to tell stories. And what a richly fascinating story the revision of the Sacramentary would make. But the time is not yet right. As of this writing, the Roman review of the Sacramentary is just under way. Over the past year [1998] the English-speaking conferences of bishops have submitted the revised text to Rome along with their decrees of approval. The Roman process that will end, it is hoped, with the confirmation of the bishops' conferences' acts of approval is still some way off. And so, the first reason why a history is not called for. It's too soon for a history of the revision of the Sacramentary. In addition, that it is not the task given to this writer according to the editors' plan for this volume of essays in honor of Dom Anscar Chupungco. The assigned task is to provide an account of the process that the International Commission on English in the Liturgy (ICEL) has followed in revising the Sacramentary. How did ICEL go about this massive, and yes, historic, undertaking? What follows is more or less a chronology, a straightforward narrative about the process, the consultations, the committees, the scholarly background preparation, the many drafts, the public reports, the voting within ICEL and, finally, within the conferences of bishops.

1

In 1981 ICEL began to make plans for the revision of the first English-language Sacramentary, completed in 1973. Certainly no one who was involved in the 1981 planning stage expected the work to take seventeen years. Ten, perhaps, twelve years, but hardly almost two decades. A true historical account would go some way to explaining how a projected ten-year work stretched on to seventeen. It would provide the opportunity for filling in the many important, even dramatic, details. But again, the current task must proceed more along the lines of "then," "after that," and "next." An occasional aside may tempt the writer and he may indulge it, but the primary emphasis will be on the plan and the process. It is hoped that this introductory essay will provide the focus for the more detailed articles on particular aspects of the Sacramentary revision which follow.

THE BIRTH OF ICEL

Perhaps before answering the question how did ICEL go about revising the Sacramentary, there is a need to look briefly at the prior question—why did ICEL decide to revise the 1973 Sacramentary? This will take us back not seventeen years, but thirty-five. Back to 4 December 1963, when Paul VI together with the more than two thousand bishops assembled in Rome solemnly promulgated the first enactment of the Second Vatican Council, *Sacrosanctum concilium*, the Constitution on the Liturgy. The formal vote taken that day was 2,147 bishops in favor, four opposed. For the purposes of this essay two elements of the liturgy constitution deserve underscoring. The first occurs in article 22 where the first conciliar mention is made of "various kinds of competent territorial bodies of bishops lawfully established," a somewhat ungainly phrase, but soon after and since, more simply, the "conferences of bishops." The second matter, and equal in pertinence, comes just a bit later, article 36, which after stating "particular law remaining in force, the use of the Latin language is to be preserved in the Latin rites" goes on to give those "various kinds of competent territorial bodies of bishops lawfully established" the authority to decide the extent to which the vernacular could be used in the celebration of the liturgy (subject to the review of the Apostolic See) and the authority to approve the vernacular texts for use in their territories. As Father Anscar Chupungco has written: "The decision of Vatican II to allow the use of the vernacular is surely one of its precious gifts," and "the translation of liturgical texts is perhaps the most delicate matter arising from the Council's decision to shift from Latin to the vernacular languages."[1]

In the previous year, soon after their arrival in Rome for the opening of the council, a small group of bishops from English-speaking countries had gathered informally to discuss their hopes for the use of the vernacular in the liturgy. They even went a step further by entertaining the possibility of a common English text to be used wherever English is spoken. As the first session of the council unfolded and the debates gave promise of at least some degree of the use of the vernacular, these bishops carried their plan to bishops from more and more conferences. By the time the bishops left Rome in early December 1962, it appeared that ten conferences of bishops where English is spoken were interested in exploring the possibility of shared common English texts. When the bishops reassembled in Rome the following autumn, the ten conferences were ready to send delegates to a meeting that would inaugurate a "mixed commission" for the preparation of liturgical texts in English. On 17 October more than a dozen bishops met at the English College and laid the groundwork for what was to become known as the International Commission on English in the Liturgy. When the liturgy constitution was adopted by the council seven weeks later, the English-speaking world was ready. Over the course of 1964 concrete form was given to the first hopes and proposals, and the ten conferences of bishops[2] gave to their international committee the formal mandate that governs the work to this day.

THE FIRST STAGE OF REVISION

The early years of ICEL saw a steady flow of English ritual books based on the Latin editions revised in the years immediately following the council by the Consilium for the Implementation of the Constitution on the Sacred Liturgy. The first work of ICEL was done with care, scholarship, and extensive consultation, but understandably there was a certain pressure to make the liturgical texts, particularly the texts of the Mass, available as soon as possible, to move beyond the interim texts that were used as an expedient when the vernacular went into effect on the First Sunday of Lent 1965. (These interim texts

1. Anscar J. Chupungco, O.S.B., "The Translation of Liturgical Texts," Anscar J. Chupungco, O.S.B., ed., *Handbook for Liturgical Studies,* Introduction to the Liturgy (Collegeville: The Liturgical Press, 1997) 1:382, 388.

2. An eleventh conference, the Philippines, was joined to the original membership in 1967.

were taken largely from existing translations, especially from hand missals for popular use in following the Latin Mass.)

By 1973 ICEL had completed its work on the first edition of the Sacramentary (The Roman Missal)[3] in English. Through 1974–75 this pioneering work had been approved by the eleven member conferences of bishops. As work on the Sacramentary was nearing completion, the Advisory Committee of ICEL recommended to ICEL's Episcopal Board that the Sacramentary be introduced for a limited period, perhaps five years, *ad experimentum.* The bishops, however, thought that there had already been too long a period of interim books and that to extend this for an additional period would not be pastorally wise. It seemed better to look toward a future revision when the liturgical reform had taken deeper root at the parish level.

By the late 1970s ICEL had provided translations of the more than twenty revised liturgical books that had been issued by Rome over the past decade, including the Sacramentary and the four-volume Liturgy of the Hours. There was then an opportunity for ICEL to pause and reflect on what had been accomplished, to weigh, at least in a preliminary form, successes and defects and to begin preparation for a deeper, more intense phase of the liturgical renewal through a second generation of English liturgical books.[4] (This type of reflection has been carried on by other major language groups as well, and the Holy See has itself issued second editions, *editiones alterae,* of a number of the early books, notably the *Missale Romanum* of 1975, the *Ordo*

3. The *Missale Romanum* of 1570 contained both the prayers of the Mass and the prescribed readings from Scripture, the epistle, and gospel. The postconciliar reform not only gave the Church a new order of Scripture readings, but also restored the practice of a distinct liturgical book for the proclamation of the readings. This created the question of how best to recognize that the *Missale* is now in practice two distinct books—a book containing the prayers proclaimed by the celebrant and another the readings proclaimed by the celebrant and other ministers. The *Ordo Lectionum Missae,* published in English in 1970, was given the title, *Lectionary for Mass.* In 1973 ICEL proposed that the celebrant's book of prayers be designated according to the ancient usage, the Sacramentary. Some English-speaking conferences adopted the title Sacramentary, others, *The Roman Missal.* With the revision of 1998 ICEL has again proposed the title *Sacramentary.*

4. Encouragement for this second phase of the liturgical renewal is given in the Holy See's 1969 Instruction on the Translation of Liturgical Texts for Celebrations with a Congregation and is also emphasized by Pope John Paul II in his 4 December 1988 apostolic letter *Vicesimus quintus annus,* on the occasion of the twenty-fifth anniversary of *Sacrosanctum concilium,* no. 20.

Lectionum Missae of 1981, the *Ordo Celebrandi Matrimonium* of 1989, and the *De Ordinatione Episcopi, Presbyterorum, et Diaconorum* of 1990.)

In 1977 the Episcopal Board of ICEL had approved a comprehensive program of revision expected to take two to three decades to complete. Each rite would be considered separately, with work beginning on the next rite only when work on the revision under way was well advanced. The work would be done steadily and deliberately. Full public consultation with the eleven member and fifteen associate-member conferences would be the first step toward the revision of each rite. All responses to the consultation, whether indicating positive or negative responses to the texts from the first generation, would be exactingly studied and reviewed. As part of its own internal preparation for the work of revision, ICEL would engage in careful research, particularly on the history and vocabulary of the Latin texts found in the postconciliar ritual books.

THE SECOND STAGE OF REVISION BEGINS

The first book selected for revision was the relatively brief *Rite of Funerals,* which had been published in 1971. The public consultation on its revision took place in 1981. The review of the responses followed in 1982. After completion of this review the revision began. The work was greatly aided by a new set of structures put into place by ICEL from the mid-1970s. While the Episcopal Board remained the ultimate authority and director for the work and while the Advisory Committee remained the steering and coordinating body for work in progress, three standing subcommittees were set up to undertake the task of preparing the various elements needed for a second generation of liturgical books. The subcommittees worked under the Advisory Committee and were closely tied to it by having a member of the Advisory Committee serve as the chairperson for each of the subcommittees. The subcommittees established were: translations and original texts, the presentation of texts, and music. (Early in the revision of the Sacramentary, the work of original or newly composed texts would be separated out of the translations subcommittee and given over to a new standing subcommittee with sole responsibility for the preparation of new texts.)

Taking one of the quantitatively smaller rites as the beginning of the revision program proved to be a wise step. Many of the lessons learned and decisions made in the funeral rite revision turned out to be applicable to the far more complex second step in the revision program, the revision of the Sacramentary. Thorough discussions on such issues as the approach to the translated texts—the spare, direct style of the first generation ICEL texts versus a fuller, more heightened style—or on the right tone and length for pastoral introductions as supplements to the Roman introduction had characterized every step of the revision of the funeral rite. While the revision of the Sacramentary obviously brought up a host of new questions, crucial matters related to the underlying principles of the ICEL second generation texts had largely been solved by the time work on the revision of the Sacramentary began in earnest.

THE REVISION OF THE SACRAMENTARY— THE FIRST CONSULTATION

The first consultation book issued for the Sacramentary revision was dated 4 October 1982. The consultation instrument dealt with the revision of the presidential prayers of the Sacramentary. The vast majority of these are the opening prayers, the prayers over the gifts, and the prayers after Communion. Two thousand books were printed by ICEL and sent to the twenty-six sponsoring and participating conferences of bishops. The consultation book contained a selection of opening prayers, prayers over the gifts, and prayers after Communion taken from all sections of the Sacramentary—the proper of seasons, the sanctoral, the commons, the ritual Masses, and the Masses and prayers for various needs and occasions. In addition to collect-style prayers, the Exsultet, the Blessing of Water, and some examples of solemn blessings were given. Each sample provided the Latin text and the 1973 ICEL translation. Respondents were invited to go beyond the sample texts given in the consultation books in submitting their comments on what the revised texts should look like. Two notable elements of the consultation book were its full introduction, which included a carefully balanced presentation of the positive and negative reactions to the 1973 Sacramentary texts, and a brief concluding questionnaire that sought information on questions such as the desirability of additional original or newly composed prayers,[5] the layout of certain sections, such as the ritual Masses, to help the celebrant to choose more easily from the various options, and a request for names of people who might be inter-

---

5. The 1973 Sacramentary contained over one hundred such texts, most notably the alternative opening prayers for Sundays and solemnities.

ested in assisting in the work of revising the Sacramentary. A year's time was given to allow respondents to prepare and submit their comments.

By early 1984 ICEL had received one hundred forty responses. Some responses were very brief; others extended to many pages. Some respondents made general remarks on what they thought was needed in the revisions; others in addition to their remarks gave examples of the style the revised texts should emulate. In some ways the limited response was disappointing, but at the same time the response received came from all parts of the world and included comments from bishops, parish priests, and laypeople. Some of those commenting provided very scholarly and well-researched analyses; others said that they felt unable to make comments on translation issues but wished to make pastoral observations that they hoped would be helpful in the revision. It should be noted also that while a number of the responses were from individuals there were in addition responses representing groups of people, usually national or diocesan liturgical commissions. In fact, then, as many as three hundred people had participated in the reflection on and preparation of comments aimed at influencing the planned revision.

The results of the consultation were tabulated, coded, and studied in a preliminary way in the ICEL secretariat over the course of 1984. Several staff members assisted in this process, but the primary person responsible for assembling the responses was Dr. Thomas C. O'Brien, who provided the scholarly underpinning needed to revise the translated texts of the Sacramentary from 1983 until his death in 1991. Before the responses to the 1982–83 consultation had been received, Dr. O'Brien had begun a massive project—background research on each of the texts of the 1969 *Missale Romanum*, especially the provenance and vocabulary of the prayers. Dr. O'Brien's studies were of immense help to the revisers with whom he worked closely over seven years. An enduring result of Dr. O'Brien's research is *A Lexicon of Terms in the Missale Romanum*, which contains 663 entries and runs to 415 pages.

When the 1982–83 consultation had been evaluated, it was clear that a majority of those responding thought that the presidential prayers needed total recasting rather than minor revisions. The Advisory Committee accepted this judgment and proposed a total revision of the collect prayers to the Episcopal Board. The bishops gave their approval to this course of action.

The fairly swift acceptance of the need for full revision was not surprising. As has been noted, when the first step in the ICEL revisions program, the revision of the *Rite of Funerals,* was taken, consideration had to be given early on to the style of the revised translated texts. There was debate within the Advisory Committee, with some members proposing that ICEL remain with the spare, direct language and paratactic structure that had characterized the first generation of ICEL texts and others calling for a fuller, richer language with a more literal approach to the Latin, both in vocabulary and syntax. Certainly each side saw the overarching need to have prayer texts suited for public proclamation rather than private reading, texts that could be easily spoken and heard. In the end those looking for a more heightened style were in the majority. This was in no sense seen to be a repudiation of the first work. It was readily agreed by all that the collect-style prayers of the pioneering stage had made an enormous contribution to the Roman Catholic Church's first English vernacular experience.[6] The first generation of texts made the claim for a liturgical language that was solid, accessible, and contemporary. The pioneering translators had clearly seen that if the language of the liturgy was to be truly living, the language of the whole of God's people at prayer, it was necessary to move away from an older diction that was too often ornate, recondite, and artificial. This type of language had gained sway in Roman Catholic English devotional prayers, often no more hallowed than a century's time, and in the English translations found in the Sunday and daily Missals that many Catholics used in an effort "to pray the Mass" along with the priest.

With the revision of the first generation of ICEL texts there was now the chance to move to a further level—language that was indeed meant for public proclamation but that was also noticeably different from everyday speech, a language that was formal yet clear, majestic but not mannered, prayerful but not ritualistic. In a sense, the revisers of the funeral rite had anticipated the results of the consultation on the collects of the 1973 Sacramentary. ICEL's own internal discus-

---

6. It is, of course, true that vernacular translations of elements of the *Rituale Romanum* had been authorized by the Apostolic See in the mid-1950s, and certainly the style of these texts had an influence on the postconciliar English texts, but the number of vernacular texts of the 1950s was very small indeed when measured against the total vernacular experience begun by the council and completed by decisions of Pope Paul VI.

sions (and in fact these had begun in the late 1970s before the revisions program had been decided on) had reached a conclusion very similar to that of the majority of respondents to the 1982–83 consultation. The way ahead was clear as the work of revising the presidential prayers began in earnest in 1984—total revision of the presidential prayers was the aim of those entrusted with the work.

A matter that came up with some frequency in the 1982–83 consultation was a request for alternative opening prayers related to the Scripture readings. Such texts had begun by the early 1980s to appear in the Sacramentaries of other language groups, most notably the revised *Messale Romano* of 1983. There was vigorous discussion within ICEL on the desirability of prayers related to the day's Scripture readings. Some thought that having opening prayers that contained echoes of the readings would not be helpful since they would be prayed before the readings were proclaimed. Others considered such opening prayers to be of value because they would bring a greater number of images from Scripture into the liturgical texts. The echoes or allusions could be a good preparation for the readings, but the basic concern was to provide a number of rich, solid alternative opening prayers. The Scriptures seemed an excellent source for composing prayers to suit this goal. A decision was made to test further the desirability of this form of collect, and in July 1983 ICEL issued a limited number of Scripture-related opening prayers for comment. A further consultation along these lines was sent to the conferences in October 1986. The responses to both consultations were strongly positive, and from 1987 ICEL committed itself to going ahead with providing opening prayers that took their inspiration from the readings for Sundays and solemnities, particularly the gospel readings.[7]

THE SECOND CONSULTATION

In March 1986 the second ICEL consultation book on the revision of the Sacramentary was sent to the conferences. The focus of this consultation was on the texts of the Order of Mass including the prefaces and Eucharistic Prayers. Again, the Latin as well as samples of the

7. Bringing further scriptural images into the Church's prayer seems particularly welcome at a time when Catholics have become more deeply acquainted with Scripture through the postconciliar *Lectionary for Mass*, which has in turn led to Scripture study and prayer groups in many parishes. As well the creation of original texts holds the possibility of enriching the corpus of liturgical prayers in English in an idiom and imagery native to the language.

1973 English texts were provided. In the case of the Eucharistic Prayers the Latin and English for the nine anaphoras then authorized by the Holy See were given in full. Fifteen hundred consultation books were sent to the conferences of bishop. The period for response ran from March 1986 to January 1987. One hundred sixty-two responses were received. Even more than in the earlier consultation, a number of these responses were from national and diocesan liturgical commissions. Overwhelmingly the respondents expressed a need for caution in revising the texts of the Order of Mass, including the Eucharistic Prayers I–IV, since these texts had over nearly two decades become well known to celebrants as well as to the members of the assembly. The latter had also committed many of the Order of Mass texts to memory, even the full texts or large sections of Eucharistic Prayers I–IV.

In 1988 a special task force was constituted in ICEL to study the results of the responses on the Order of Mass texts. The 210-page report of the task force, completed in January 1989, supported the recommendations received from the 1986 consultation that the texts of the Order of Mass be changed only where such changes were judged to be strongly necessary. The Advisory Committee agreed with this report and the Episcopal Board accepted it, directing that in light of pastoral judgment limited changes be made in the Order of Mass texts.[8]

To ensure that revision of the Eucharistic Prayers was given an even more exacting consideration, an additional consultation was carried out in 1990 with liturgical scholars and sacramental theologians. The results from this further sounding had an important part in the decisions taken by ICEL in the revision of the Eucharistic Prayers.

THE PROGRESS REPORTS
By March 1988 ICEL was ready to issue to the conferences the first of three progress reports on the Sacramentary revision. Though largely

8. Since the Eucharistic Prayers for Masses with Children (1975) and the Eucharistic Prayers for Reconciliation (1975) had not become as well known as Eucharistic Prayers I–IV and since the Eucharistic Prayers for Masses with Children and the Eucharistic Prayers for Reconciliation were in the 1980s still in an interim form, it was agreed in ICEL that more extensive revisions of these prayers would not be pastorally insensitive. Because of the special considerations involved in revising the Eucharistic Prayers for Masses with Children, an ad hoc subcommittee involving ICEL's members but also other experts from outside ICEL prepared a working draft of the prayers for children over the course of 1991.

meant to chronicle the progress of the work for information purposes, the reports did also invite questions or comments from the conferences of bishops. The first report dealt solely with the translation of the opening prayers. A number of examples of revised texts were provided, but the report also gave considerable attention to the scholarly material prepared by ICEL to underpin the revision of the translations of the opening prayers.

The Second Progress Report followed in September 1990. This time the focus was on original prayers as well as translated texts. Examples of the newly composed opening prayers inspired by the three-year Sunday cycle of Scripture readings were given. The examples of translated texts were limited to prayers over the gifts and prayers after Communion.

The Catholic press in various parts of the English-speaking world took some notice of the first and second progress reports, but on the whole the response was minimal. Comments either positive or negative were few. ICEL had every reason then to conclude that the work was proceeding on an acceptable course, and indeed for the most part this would in retrospect prove to be a sound conclusion. The conferences of bishops, it seemed clear, were largely happy with the course the revision was taking. There was every indication that the completed revision would in the main be positively received by the conferences.

The Third Progress Report, published in April 1992, concentrated on the Order of Mass texts including the Eucharistic Prayers. It began with an important introduction that reflected on lessons learned in the nearly ten years of revising the Sacramentary. With the issuance of the third public report, the calm that had accompanied the revision and its public presentation was suddenly no longer the case in some areas of the English-speaking world. Clearly and understandably the Order of Mass texts were being given a scrutiny by some recipients of the third report in a way that was altogether different from their reaction to the two earlier ICEL reports that had concentrated principally on the collect-type prayers. In some quarters, however, it appeared that the very public process begun in October 1982 was being noticed for the first time. That ICEL had been involved in a decade-long revision of the 1973 Sacramentary was greeted here and there with considerable surprise. Public comment was strong, especially in the United States, and the revision of the Sacramentary even gained the attention of *Time* magazine in a full article in its religion section on 26 October 1992. Groups were founded in the United States to convince the bishops that the Sacramentary revision was deeply flawed. Letter-writing campaigns to bring the work to a halt were aimed at the bishops and the Roman dicasteries. While certain points made by the critics were useful and had a positive influence within ICEL on the work as it continued to move to completion, the overall effect was regrettable. Many of the considerable improvements represented by the revision over the 1973 texts were either unfairly caricatured or simply ignored. The debate chiefly centered on a few issues, inclusive language large among them. Unfortunately this atmosphere of harsh polemic would continue throughout the subsequent stages of the revision process, and beyond.

In the period 1988–92 as the progress reports were making the bishops and the rest of the wider Church aware of the actual work being accomplished, the revision within ICEL was gradually taking final shape in anticipation of presenting the revised Sacramentary to the conferences for their review and eventual canonical vote.

In addition to the revision of the close to two thousand Latin texts that were the responsibility of ICEL's subcommittee on translations and revisions and the three hundred newly composed texts that fell to the subcommittee on original texts, ICEL's subcommittee on the presentation of texts was heavily engaged with its own tasks, the layout and design of the book to ensure its effectiveness in liturgical celebration, the preparation of brief introductory notes for major days in the Roman Calendar as well as all the saints' days, the plan for certain "variations" called for by the consultation with the conferences, such as a moderate simplification of the introductory rites of Mass, and the preparation of pastoral introductions for the major sections of the Sacramentary—the liturgical seasons, the sanctoral, the commons, and the like. The most extended pastoral introduction was written for the Order of Mass. This introduction was in no sense meant as a replacement of the General Instruction of the Roman Missal, but clearly intended as a supplement to underscore in strongly pastoral terms for all the ministers involved in the eucharistic celebration, especially the Sunday celebration, the need to be attentive to the norms of the General Instruction. The pastoral introduction for the Order of Mass was a work of seven years and went though fifteen drafts before it was considered ready to present to the conferences of bishops.

THE REVISION AND MUSIC

There was less work for ICEL's music subcommittee in the first years of the revision. The subcommittee had necessarily to wait until the texts—collects, prefaces, Eucharistic Prayers, solemn blessings—were in advanced draft form before applying the chant tones to them. While waiting for the texts to be ready, the music subcommittee carefully studied criticisms of the 1973 Sacramentary chants and developed principles to guide in overcoming these defects when the revision began. Obviously once the music subcommittee had the revised texts in hand, dialogue with the translations and original texts subcommittees was necessary. This dialogue led to some textual changes to accommodate the requirements of the chant tones. When the texts had been set to music, the subcommittee carried on a consultation with over two hundred musicians, chiefly experts in Gregorian chant, from all over the English-speaking world. A number of changes were made in the chant tones in response to the critiques received from those consulted.

A special ad hoc subcommittee involving members of the subcommittees on music and translations was established in 1992 to prepare the texts of the entrance and communion antiphons as well as the hymn texts in the Sacramentary, for example, the *Pange lingua*, the *Crux fidelis*, and the *O Redemptor*. Great care was given to the antiphons to ensure their singability, with the hope that musical compositions would reinvigorate the use of the antiphons, especially in Sunday and other major celebrations, as true processional songs.

THE STEERING COMMITTEE

With several different groups assigned the task of revising the Sacramentary some mechanism had to be put in place to ensure that all the pieces were falling into place. While the ICEL Advisory Committee continued to be the overall steering and coordinating group throughout the project, it was clear by 1992 that a special steering committee was needed to keep the various groups in dialogue with each other and to settle questions of overlapping responsibilities as the work began to take final shape. The steering committee was made up of the chair of the Advisory Committee and the chairs of the four standing subcommittees.

The work of the Advisory Committee was heavy, demanding, and crucial from 1983 onward. (And it should be recalled that ICEL was engaged in other needed tasks during the years of the Sacramentary revision—the *Collection of Masses in Honor of the Blessed Virgin Mary,* the *Book of Blessings,* the *Ceremonial of Bishops,* the translation of the psalter and biblical canticles for study and comment, and the revisions of the marriage rite and ordination rites occasioned by the Roman *editiones alterae* of these books, 1989 and 1990 respectively.) The work of the Advisory Committee became even heavier in the late 1980s and early 1990s as the various sections of the revised Sacramentary came before it for the final votes that would allow the work to go forward to the Episcopal Board.

THE WORK OF THE EPISCOPAL BOARD

Over the entire revision period the board of bishops had received written reports on the work in progress, and during their annual meetings full oral reports on the Sacramentary revision had the primary place on the bishops' agenda. At every stage the board gave its approval to the work under way and indeed its encouragement. At various points before the formal voting period the bishops made decisions on certain special questions. In 1990 the board of bishops canvassed the conferences concerning the proposed modest reordering of the introductory rites of the Order of Mass. In addition, the ICEL Episcopal Board consulted the conferences on the use of the word "presbyter" instead of "priest" in the titles and texts of the revised Sacramentary. This matter was raised in light of the distinction made by the Holy See in the 1968 *De Ordinatione* between the *munus episcopi* and the *munus presbyteri* within the single *sacerdotium.* In 1993 the board authorized a consultation on the translation of the words *et homo factus est* in the Nicene Creed. (The 1988 translation had been prepared by the ecumenical body, the English Language Liturgical Consultation.) From early in the Sacramentary revision a proposal had been under consideration on whether the revised Sacramentary should be presented in a single volume or in two volumes. The Advisory Committee decided in favor of proposing a two-volume arrangement, along the lines of the German *Messbuch,* volume one for Sundays and solemnities, volume two for weekdays. The Episcopal Board agreed to the two-volume arrangement.

By June 1991 the first "batch" of texts was ready for the vote of the Episcopal Board. Nine would follow through August 1995. In several instances the bishop representative on the Episcopal Board invited other bishops in his conference to join him in reviewing the revised material in preparation for his vote. The handling of negative and *iuxta modum* votes returned by members of the Episcopal Board required the establishment of yet another special committee, the editorial committee. The members, again taken from the Advisory Committee and subcommittees, met to consider each negative and *iuxta modum* vote. In the few instances when the editorial committee decided to recommend against accepting a negative or *iuxta modum* vote of a member of the board, the committee drew up a report giving its reasons, and this was then submitted for final decision to the three-member executive committee of the Episcopal Board.

APPROVAL OF THE CONFERENCES OF BISHOPS
As the Episcopal Board began its voting process, plans were also under discussion for the presentation of the revised Sacramentary to the conferences of bishops. There was a major question—whether to present the Sacramentary for the conferences' canonical vote by volume, one and two, or in segments. The first plan—the fully arranged books as intended for actual celebration—would have been easier from ICEL's point of view. The presentation of segments would mean a disassembling of the whole and then a reassembling at the end of the conferences' voting process. It soon became clear, however, that the conferences would find the enormous task of voting easier if the material was presented in segments. The conference of bishops of the United States formally asked ICEL to submit the revised Sacramentary in segments, and ICEL immediately responded by developing a plan for sending the revision to the conferences by segments. The segments were presented to the conferences as follows: Ordinary Time, September 1993; Proper of Seasons, April 1994; Order of Mass I, August 1994; Order of Mass II, February 1995; the Sanctoral, May 1995; Holy Week, August 1995; Common of Saints, Ritual Masses, Votive Masses, and Masses for the Dead, February 1996; Various Needs and Occasions, August 1996.

At the completion of the conferences' voting, 192 texts had been returned to ICEL for reconsideration. Again, the editorial committee reviewed the "remanded" texts in the first instance and, after discussion, sent on their recommendations to the executive committee of the Episcopal Board for final decision.

In December 1997 ICEL sent to the national liturgical commissions of the conferences the Sacramentary assembled for the first time in the two-volume arrangement. The two volumes had not yet been finally edited by ICEL but were intended to assist the commissions in

15

preparing for each conference's submission of the revised Sacramentary to Rome. Five months later the finally edited version of the revised Sacramentary was sent to the twenty-six conferences of bishops that participate in ICEL. ICEL's work of preparing the second English edition of the Sacramentary had after seventeen years come to this decisive, though perhaps not yet final, stage. Hopes for the implementation of the revised Sacramentary in the parishes of the English-speaking world during the Jubilee Year continue.

Gilbert Ostdiek, O.F.M.

Principles of Translation
in the Revised Sacramentary

"If I translate word by word, it sounds absurd; if I am forced to change something in the word order or style, I seem to have stopped being a translator." Commenting on this dilemma posed by one of the most celebrated translators in our Christian tradition, Anscar Chupungco writes:

"With these words St. Jerome articulated the experience of every conscientious translator. Word-by-word translation often does not make sense, but a change in the meaning of the word betrays the message. The translation of liturgical texts is perhaps the most delicate and complex matter arising from the Church's decision to shift from Latin to the vernacular languages."[1]

On what principles does one proceed in such a delicate and complex matter? To explore that question posed by Chupungco's comment this essay will look at principles which have gradually developed in the wake of that momentous decision, namely: (1) the pastoral principle underlying the conciliar decision to restore the vernacular;[2] (2) the guidelines set forth in the 1969 *Instruction* issued by the Consilium,

1. A. Chupungco, "The Translation of Liturgical Texts," *Handbook for Liturgical Studies: Introduction to the Liturgy,* ed. A. Chupungco (Collegeville: The Liturgical Press, 1997) 1:388. It gives me great pleasure to contribute this essay to a volume honoring Fr. Anscar Chupungco, O.S.B., on the occasion of his sixtieth birthday. He is a loyal friend and an esteemed colleague in the work of ICEL.

2. For the decision, see Vatican II, Constitution on the Sacred Liturgy (*Sacrosanctum concilium* 36, 54, 63); hereafter cited as SC.

the Roman commission established to oversee the implementation of the liturgical reforms of Vatican II;[3] and (3) a sample of the working principles used by the International Commission on English in the Liturgy (ICEL) in revising the Sacramentary.[4] The essay will conclude with several reflections on the art of translation.

THE PASTORAL PRINCIPLE OF VATICAN II

The fundamental principle guiding the entire Vatican II reform of the liturgy is succinctly stated in the Constitution on the Sacred Liturgy (*Sacrosanctum concilium*, hereafter, SC): "In the reform and promotion of the liturgy, this full and active participation by all the people is the aim to be considered before all else" (SC 14). Toward this end, the council directed that a number of pastoral actions be taken, including a reform of the rites themselves, a richer use of Scripture, liturgical formation of clergy and people, and a return to the use of the vernacular in liturgical celebrations. Though Vatican II had envisioned only a limited use of the vernacular (SC 36, 54, 63), within a few years after the council Rome approved requests from numerous episcopal conferences to extend the use of modern languages beyond the readings and general intercessions to all the prayers of the Mass.

Although this decision to return to the vernacular caught many in the Church by surprise, it was not without precedent. The early community probably used Aramaic when it gathered for Eucharist. And as Christianity spread into the hellenized areas of the Mediterranean, including Rome, Christians adopted a form of everyday Greek called *koine* as their language of prayer. Textual evidence dates the adoption of Latin in the Eucharistic Prayer to between 360 and 382.[5] The de-

3. Consilium, *Instruction on the Translation of Liturgical Texts for Celebrations with a Congregation.* See *Documents on the Liturgy 1963–1979* (Collegeville: The Liturgical Press, 1982) 284–91 (DOL 838–80). This document, though often identified by the French title, *Comme le prévoit,* was issued simultaneously in six major modern languages and will be cited hereafter as *Instruction.*

4. A fuller listing and description of these principles with accompanying documentation can be found in "An Interim Report on the ICEL Revision of the Sacramentary, 1982–1994," which ICEL made available to its Episcopal Board and the national liturgy secretariats of member conferences.

5. See T. Klauser, *A Short History of the Western Liturgy: An Account and Some Reflections* (New York: Oxford University Press, 1979) 18–19; C. Mohrmann, *Liturgical Latin: Its Origins and Character* (Washington, D.C.: The Catholic

finitive transition from Greek to Latin is attributed to the pontificate of Damasus I (d. 384), and it was from the fourth to the late sixth century that liturgical Latin developed.[6] During that time the corpus of "collects," the prayers proclaimed by the presider as the concluding ritual element of three processions in the fully developed basilican liturgy—entrance, presentation of gifts, and Communion—gradually took shape. Originally improvised oral texts, these collects were eventually gathered in written form to become a body of fixed texts. Bishops of Rome such as Innocent (d. 417), Leo the Great (d. 461), Gelasius (d. 521), Vigilius (d. 555), and Gregory the Great (d. 604) were among the chief authors.

The point to be drawn from these brief historical notes is that both the Eucharistic Prayer and the collects were not translations of preceding texts. They were original compositions. That is, they were a free wording of familiar themes within a known prayer structure or pattern. By the time of Vatican II, some fifteen hundred years later, they had become fixed formulae handed on by ancient tradition. In its decision to return to contemporary vernacular the council assumed that the texts of the reformed liturgy would for the most part be translations of these ancient Latin prayers (or of Latin prayers newly formed from them by the "mosaic" principle), not original compositions as those Latin prayers had been. On both scores, then, the international mixed commissions established for this purpose were left with a daunting task: to learn at one and the same time the art of translating prayers from Latin and of shaping a contemporary style of liturgical prayer in the vernacular. For this task, the basic pastoral principle of Vatican II provided little guidance other than to lay stress on the importance of enabling today's assemblies to pray in their mother tongue. Guidelines were yet to be worked out, even as the demanding work of translating some two thousand texts of the Sacramentary got underway. The next two sections will trace some of that subsequent development of guidelines.

A factor which further complicates the task of translation should first be noted. From ancient times the Latin collects were called *orationes*,

University of America Press, 1957) 50; C. Vogel, *Medieval Liturgy: An Introduction to the Sources* (Washington, D.C.: The Pastoral Press, 1986) 295–97.

6. A. Chupungco, "The Cultural and Domestic Tradition of the Eucharist," *Worship: Progress and Tradition* (Washington, D.C.: The Pastoral Press, 1995) 26.

which Emminghaus translates as "prayer-speech."[7] That is, they were proclaimed; they were to be heard and not read by the assembly. So the authors shaped these texts for proclamation in a large public space, using the rhetorical devices of the cultured Latin of their day, such as the rhythm called *cursus,* binary parallelism, antithesis, and the balanced symmetry called *concinnitas.*[8] The resulting prayers were stately, restrained, and concise, with the literary qualities of public, cultured Latin. They were not cast in the popular Latin of everyday and the marketplace. Accordingly, Chupungco reasons, this kind of highly cultivated Latin, "demanded by the solemn ambit of the Roman basilica," was "accessible almost exclusively to the educated segment of the Roman Church."[9] But contrary to the position taken earlier by Mohrmann,[10] he also argues that liturgical language, then and now, should not be seen as a sacred language. Rather, it is ritual language which is to be both literary and accessible to the majority of the assembly.[11] The added question for translators today, then, is whether the classical rhetorical style and techniques of these Latin texts are to be brought over intact into the vernacular text (*translatio* literally means to "bring over" from a source language into a receptor language). Can full participation of the assembly be achieved with that kind of rhetorical style, or must another language register be found? If so, what principles are to be followed?

GUIDELINES OF THE 1969 INSTRUCTION

The first full set of guidelines for the work of translation was issued by the Consilium in 1969.[12] Chupungco has noted that in many ways

---

7. J. Emminghaus, *The Eucharist: Form, Essence, Celebration* (Collegeville: The Liturgical Press, 1978) 128.

8. For fuller explanation, see A. Chupungco, "Ritual Language and Liturgy," *Finding Voice to Give God Praise: Essays in the Many Languages of the Liturgy,* ed. K. Hughes (Collegeville: The Liturgical Press, 1998) 92–93.

9. Chupungco, "The Cultural and Domestic Tradition," 29.

10. Mohrmann, *Liturgical Latin,* 60–90.

11. Chupungco, "Ritual Language and Liturgy," 91.

12. These guidelines are still in effect and govern the work of ICEL and the other international commissions. Rome is reportedly working on another set of guidelines. To date there has been no indication of when the new document will be issued, what the contents will be, or whether it will supplement or supplant the 1969 *Instruction.* Regrettably, the new guidelines are being developed in Rome without the benefit of the broad, international collaboration and experience that marked the preparation of the 1969 *Instruction.* For his-

the 1969 *Instruction* can be seen as an elaboration of what Pope Paul VI had already said in an address to translators of liturgical texts gathered in Rome in November of 1965. Chupungco summarizes three basic principles running through the Pope's address as follows. First, the principle aim of translation, as the council had said, is to promote the active participation of the assembly. It was for this reason, Paul noted, that the Church was willing to let go of its centuries-old Latin liturgy. What is to be gained from this sacrifice is that the new vernacular texts are "within the grasp of all, even children and the uneducated." Second, the translated texts are no longer simply aids "to assist the faithful's understanding of the rite celebrated in Latin" by the priest. Now they "have become part of the rites themselves; they have become the voice of the Church." Third, the language used in the liturgy "should always be worthy of the noble realities it signifies, set apart from everyday speech of the street and the marketplace." A "clarity of language and dignity of expression" similar to that of the Latin texts should shine forth in the vernacular prayers.[13]

These guidelines were worked out in more detail in the 1969 *Instruction*. The Consilium notes that the purpose of the document is to lay down some of the more important theoretical and practical principles to guide the work (4). The principles are given in common and nontechnical terms; the document does not enter into a discussion of theory. Section I, entitled "General Principles," contains the guidelines that concern us here. An extended summary follows.[14]

Paragraphs 5–7 of Section I set down three broad principles: liturgical texts are a medium of spoken communication (5); the purpose of these texts is "to proclaim the message of salvation and to express the prayer of the Church to the Lord" (6); and translations "must be faithful to the art of communication in all its aspects" (7).

---

torical details on the development of the *Instruction*, see A. Bugnini, *The Reform of the Liturgy: 1948–1975* (Collegeville: The Liturgical Press, 1990) esp. chs. 9 and 16; J. Gelineau, "Quelques remarques en marge de l'Instruction sur le traduction des textes liturgiques," *La Maison-Dieu* 98 (1969) 156–62.

13. Chupungco, "The Translation of Liturgical Texts," 386–87. Phrases in quotation marks are taken from the translation of Pope Paul's address found in DOL 786–90.

14. This summary draws extensively on what I have written in "Instruction on the Translation of Liturgical Texts: A Commentary," *FDLC Newsletter* 21 (2) (March–April 1994) 9–14, 15, 16.

Two further comments are in order. Paragraph 6 sets the goal and tenor for the work of translation:

"To achieve this end, it is not sufficient that a liturgical translation merely reproduce the expressions and ideas of the original text. Rather, it must faithfully communicate to a given people, and in their own language, that which the Church by means of this given text originally intended to communicate to another people in another time. A faithful translation, therefore, cannot be judged on the basis of individual words: the total context of this specific act of communication must be kept in mind, as well as the literary form proper to the respective language."

Paragraph 7 states that the fidelity demanded of liturgical texts is threefold: to the message communicated, to the intended audience, and to the manner of expression. To insist on what the *Instruction* elsewhere calls "mere verbal fidelity" without regard for these more important kinds of fidelity would be to miss the point. The preliminary Latin text of the *Instruction* offers us a clue to the importance of these three aspects of faithful translation by lettering them ABC and making them the topical divisions for the remainder of this section.

Paragraphs 8–13 take up (A) fidelity to the message. The *Instruction* notes first that even though the message cannot be separated from the manner of speaking, first consideration is to be given to translating the meaning (8). This requires the use of established scientific methods of textual study (9): establishing the best critical text and making it the basis for the translation (10); studying the meaning of the Latin terms in light of their uses (11); not letting an analytical concern for particular phrases draw the translator away from the meaning of the whole passage (12); and keeping the meaning of words and expressions in their proper historical, social, and ritual contexts (13). The principle enunciated in paragraph 12, that the "'unit of meaning' is not the individual word but the whole passage," is of particular importance for translation.

Paragraphs 14–24 address (B) fidelity to the intended audience. The fidelity and accuracy of a translation can be assessed only in terms of the goal of serving a particular congregation (14). Accordingly, three points follow. First, the language chosen should be in common usage (15); second, several other principles concerning choice of language are to be followed to insure that hearers understand the revealed truths expressed in the liturgy (16), namely: religious language borrowed from common usage should be able to bear a Christian meaning (17); the nearest suitable words should be chosen from common language if there are none that correspond exactly (18); and a biblical or liturgical language may have to be created, by infusing Christian meaning into common words (19). The third point regarding fidelity to the audience is worth quoting in full:

"The prayer of the Church is always the prayer of some actual community, assembled here and now. It is not sufficient that a formula handed down from some other time or region be translated verbatim, even if accurately, for liturgical use. The formula translated must become the genuine prayer of the congregation and in it each member should be able to find and express himself or herself" (20).

This means that translations will require adaptation in varying degrees (21): word-for-word translations sometimes suffice (22); sometimes a change of metaphor is required to preserve the original meaning (23); and when the meaning can no longer be understood for various reasons, other ways must be found to express it in modern words (24).

Together these paragraphs insist on a register, vocabulary, and style of liturgical language that allow the assembly full access to the liturgy and the mysteries it celebrates. As the preliminary Latin text of the *Instruction* notes, no translation is *bona 'in se'*; it is more or less good only to the degree that it enables a given assembly to participate fully in the liturgy and to make the prayers their own. The crafting of common language into words suitable to voice the prayer of the local assembly is a second key demand of total fidelity.

Paragraphs 25–29 look briefly at (C) fidelity to the spoken or rhetorical style. This is of major importance for the translator of liturgical texts (25). Two things are to be noted: first, the genre of every liturgical text (acclamation, supplication, proclamation, etc.) affects the choice of words (26); and second, received written texts must be examined to discover the significant rhetorical elements proper to each (27). Some such elements are essential, others secondary; essential elements are to be preserved, whether intact or in equivalent terms (28). And finally, qualities essential to a given genre (e.g., the intelligibility of prayers said aloud) may take precedence over qualities less significant for communication (e.g., verbal fidelity) (29).

Though the *Instruction* espouses fully the importance of effective proclamatory style in the translations, these paragraphs are the least developed in terms of concrete directions. Two factors may be at work. The first is inherent in the shift to the vernacular. It is not easy to reduce the unique rhetorical needs of a half dozen modern languages to a common set of guidelines. This is compounded by another factor already indicated above. Since the late patristic period the Church has had little practice in fashioning prayer texts for full public proclamation in the living language of the assembly. Despite the remarkable progress made since Vatican II, the time has been too short for a fully mature language and rhetorical style for our prayer to take shape. It has been and continues to be a primary concern of ICEL to work out guidelines for implementing the fidelity required in the style of the new vernacular prayer. It is a work in progress that may well require several generations, as did the development of liturgical Latin. To that work we now turn.

ICEL WORKING PRINCIPLES

One of the first decisions facing ICEL was a choice of what can be called the language register.[15] To realize the magnitude of the shift of register that has taken place, we need only recall a typical preconciliar way of rendering the Latin into English in the people's hand missals of that time. In one such translation the opening prayer for Sunday XXVII in Ordinary Time reads:

"O Almighty and Eternal God, since, in the abundance of Thy loving kindness, Thou dost usually go beyond the merits and desires of Thy lowly petitioners, pour forth Thy mercy upon us both to forgive what our conscience fears and to give what our prayer would not presume to ask. Through Our Lord . . ."

Today this rendering of this prayer, taken from a widely used pocket missal edited by Fr. Joseph Stedman in 1941,[16] sounds highly mannered and archaic. Contrast that with the translation in the 1973 Sacramentary currently in use:

"Father,
your love for us

15. The following paragraphs depend in part on what I have written in "Crafting English Prayer Texts: The ICEL Revision of the Sacramentary," *Studia Liturgica* 26 (1) (1996) 128–39.
16. J. F. Stedman, *My Sunday Missal* (Brooklyn, N.Y.: Confraternity of Christian Doctrine, 1941) 254.

24

surpasses all our hopes and desires.
Forgive our failings,
keep us in your peace
and lead us in the way of salvation.
We ask this . . ."

This translation has been shortened by almost 50 percent, reducing it
to a bare minimum of two very short sentences with staccato effect.
The language has been simplified and has the feeling of ordinary
speech. Not all of the 1973 prayers are as extreme as this example,
but it does show that the early editors of ICEL were clearly striving
for an unadorned, crisp, and plain-spoken style of English. In the
light of several decades of pastoral experience, it has become apparent that this language register falls short of what the liturgy requires
if the prayers are to be fully nourishing and memorable. The 1998 revision adopted in principle a noticeably different style. The revised
translation of this prayer now reads:

"Almighty and eternal God,
whose bounty is greater than we deserve or desire,
pour out upon us your abundant mercy;
forgive the things that weigh upon our consciences
and enrich us with blessings
for which our prayers dare not hope.
We ask this . . ."

The 1998 style is fuller and more literate. It is an elevated style, sharing the heightened quality of formal public speech. The sentence
structure is now more complex; use of the relative pronoun, as in the
Latin, allows the prayer to be recast into one sentence. And overall
the prayer is far more memorable.

   This prayer can also serve to illustrate other aspects of the style
which ICEL is now working to achieve in its revisions of the various
rites. In broad strokes, it can be said that the characteristic style of a
literate language is determined by its rhythm, sound, and imagery.
Kenneth Larsen, a scholar of Elizabethan English who has been one
of the chief ICEL editors for the last three decades, has explored these
three elements further.[17]

17. See K. J. Larsen, "Language as Aural," *Worship* 54 (1980) 18–35. This article provides a good introduction to the question of the oral/aural quality of
prayer language.

Rhythm consists of a "rough pattern of speech stresses, phrases and ideas." In oral speech the rhythmic pattern of speech stresses and pauses for breathing is in effect an "audible system of punctuation" which helps hearers capture the meaning.[18] Incidentally, the use of sense lines adopted by ICEL also serves that same purpose visually for the presider. The sample prayer, with markings for strong (´) and weak (`) accents, scans as follows:

"Almíghty and etérnal Gód,
whose boúnty is greáter than we desérve or desíre,
poúr oút upón us your abúndant mércy;
forgíve the thíngs that weígh upon our cónsciencès
and enrích us with bléssings
for whìch our práyers dáre nòt hópe.
We ask this . . ."

Larsen notes that the most instinctive rhythmic pattern in English phrasing since the Middle Ages has been the use of half-lines of two speech stresses each. Applied to liturgical prayers, the attention given to rhythm in the translation process works as follows. Since English sentence structure gives the greatest weight to the end of the sentence, ICEL makes it a practice whenever possible to end every line, and especially the last line, with an accented syllable. An accent on the second last syllable is also acceptable, but every effort is made to avoid endings with several weak syllables. Larsen then counsels using what he calls the "count-back principle" to arrange units of meaning with two or three stresses each. Sense lines will then typically have two to four stresses. Only occasionally will an individual line have five speech stresses. The sample prayer illustrates this quite well.

The rhythmic pattern of English, though regular and identifiable, is nevertheless quite fluid and flexible. The Latin *cursus,* by comparison, relies on more restricted sequences of a fixed number of accented and unaccented syllables at the end of a line.[19] The English rhythmic pattern being considered here also differs from the formalized rhythm found in poetic meter. In a very few cases the ICEL prayers have consciously adopted poetic meter for specific reasons. The best example is the opening prayer for Sunday VIII in Ordinary Time:

18. Ibid., 22.
19. For an explanation of the *cursus,* see H. Leclercq, "Cursus," in *Dictionnaire d'Archéologie Chrétienne et de Liturgie* III, cols. 3193–3205.

"Direct the course of this world, Lord God,
and order it in your peace,
that your Church may serve you
in serenity and quiet joy.
We ask this . . ."

This prayer, drawn from the *Sacramentarium Veronense*, reflects the anxieties of a time when Rome was under siege and the existing world order on the verge of collapse.[20] What we hear in the content of the prayer is our instinctive human cry to God to protect us and bring order out of chaos. The revised translation (which happened to be in preparation at a time when the recent fragmentation of communist bloc countries in Eastern Europe was having its geopolitical impact) tries to capture those same sentiments in the prayer's rhythm as well. The primary meter of this prayer, commonplace in English poetry, is iambic (short-long). But two variations derived from this rhythm are also used: anapest (short-short-long) and spondee (long-long). By weaving these rhythmic variations into the pattern of the prayer, the prayer subtly embodies a larger sense of order which binds together the different rhythms, giving inarticulate expression to the very longings voiced in the words of the prayer.

To continue our comments on the previous prayer, several other elements of style might also be noted. Literate language makes judicious use of rhetorical devices such as repetition ("bounty" / "abundant"), archaisms ("bounty" with its allusion to the table grace familiar to Catholics), alliteration ("deserve or desire"), assonance ("bounty" / "abundant"), antithesis ("abundant mercy" / what we "deserve"; "things that weigh" / "blessings"), inversion (inversion of the first line to delay the address, which is then highlighted orally by the spondee meter), etc. Imagery also has a role to play in the prayer. The phrase "things that weigh upon our consciences" (*quae conscientia metuit*, literally "things which conscience fears") is a strong image which subtly suggests being bent down and brought low, implying by contrast that God's forgiveness removes the heavy burden and

20. See L. K. Mohlberg and others, ed., *Sacramentarium Veronense* (*Rerum Ecclesiasticarum Documenta, Series Maior, Fontes* 1) (Rome: Herder, 1966) 633. The prayer dates back to the winter of 537–38, when the Ostrogothic king, Witiges, was laying siege to Rome. A. Chavasse, "Messes du Pape Vigile (537–555) dans le Sacramentaire Léonien," *Ephemerides Liturgicae* 64 (1950) 183–85, ascribes the prayer to Pope Vigilius and dates it to Quinquagesima Sunday, February 14, 538.

raises us up. And the final two lines depict a striking blend of the assembly's stance of bold petition and humble deference before God.

Usually, then, translation will require that the translator find the characteristic English style and idiom which can equivalently express the message of the Latin original.[21] In some cases, however, it is possible to replicate the classical style and stateliness of the Latin more directly. The opening prayer of Sunday XVII in Ordinary Time is an example of a classical Latin text open to such replication. It reads:

"Protector in te sperantium, Deus,
sine quo nihil est validum, nihil sanctum,
multiplica super nos misericordiam tuam
ut, te rectore, te duce,
sic bonis transeuntibus nunc utamur,
ut iam possimus inhaerere mansuris.
Per Dominum."

The revised translation reads:

"O God,
protector of those who hope in you,
without you nothing is strong, nothing is holy;
enfold us in your gracious care and mercy,
that with you as our ruler and guide,
we may use wisely the gifts of this passing world
and fix our hearts even now on those which last forever.
We ask this . . ."

Other than the *cursus* for which this prayer is often used as an example, a number of favorite rhetorical devices of classical Latin

21. It should be noted that the 1969 *Instruction,* in keeping with its stated purpose of not entering into theory, does not espouse by name the approach to translation called "dynamic equivalence" (as opposed to "formal or literal equivalence"). Nevertheless, the guidelines set down in the *Instruction* clearly work on that principle. The contrast between the two approaches might be characterized as the difference between translating meaning-for-meaning and word-for-word. Today translators of both Scripture and literature generally base their work on the principle of dynamic equivalence. See, e.g., W. Barnstone, *The Poetics of Translation: History, Theory, Practice* (New Haven: Yale University Press, 1993); L. Sanneh, *Translating the Message: The Missionary Impact on Culture* (Maryknoll: Orbis, 1989). There is some recent discussion of "functional equivalence" as an alternative, in C. Hargreave, *A Translator's Freedom* (Sheffield, Eng.: Sheffield Academic Press, 1993).

found in this prayer can be matched in English: e.g., parallel expressions of the same theme ("nothing is strong, nothing is holy"); antithesis or contrast (". . . this passing world . . . even now" / "last forever"); and a balanced symmetry of words and concepts throughout the prayer as a whole *(concinnitas).* The prayer does, however, contain a striking variation on the Latin for line four *(multiplica super nos misericordiam tuam,* literally "multiply upon us your mercy"). The English "multiply" now has connotations which are too quantitative to capture the prayer's sense of the tenderhearted lavishness of God's mercy. The verb "enfold" was chosen both because it could bear that sense of God's prodigal mercy, imaged here as completely enveloping us, and because it subtly evokes our human experience of being enfolded in the embrace of another—parent, child, lover, friend, consoler— as a dim reflection of how God acts toward us. Language such as this can be of immense help in addressing the issue of how to balance gendered language for God.

The examples and comments to this point are meant to illustrate ICEL's concern for finding an English style which is faithful both to the message contained in the Latin original and to the needs of a gathered assembly which is now to make that prayer its own. These are only partial illustrations of the concerns which those working on revising the Sacramentary have brought to the table.[22] The final section will step back from this sampling of ICEL's working principles and reflect on several convictions which undergird them.

THE ART OF TRANSLATION

First, ICEL's conviction that translation is an art should be apparent from the above samples. Scientific and scholarly study are a necessary preparation for the work of translation, but it remains in the end an art. Perhaps no one has expressed this more graphically than Hilaire Belloc. In the fifth of his recommendations to translators, "to transmute boldly," he writes:

---

22. For example, four of the working principles adopted early on in the revision of the various rites were: (1) careful attention to the substantive fidelity to the Latin originals; (2) a fuller vocabulary with a greater use of adjectives and strong verbs; (3) greater attention to speech stresses, that is, the rhythm and cadence of the prayers; (4) use of connectives that result in somewhat longer sentences to convey the subordination of ideas in the text. See ICEL, "An Interim Report," appended Document 1.

"[T]he general rule should stand that, after having grasped as exactly as possible all that the original stands for, with the proportion between its various parts, the distinction between what is emphasized and what is left on a lower plane, we should say to ourselves, not 'How shall I make this foreigner talk English?' but 'What would an English [person] have said to express this same?' *That* is translation. *That* is the very essence of the art: the resurrection of an alien thing in a native body; not the dressing of it up in native clothes but the giving to it of native flesh and blood."[23]

If translation is an art, rather than a science, the principles which guide it are not to be taken as rote formulae to be applied mechanically, but as the formative discipline which shapes the translator's work just as discipline *(ascesis)* in their arts shapes the performance of the poet and the actor.

Second, ICEL working principles embody the conviction that the translated texts are first and foremost meant to be the prayer of the gathered assembly, proclaimed and heard in faith. The oral/aural quality of these prayers demands that they be cast in ways of speaking that are both accessible to all, yet worthy of revealing the holy mystery they announce. The need to be attentive to fidelity to the Latin text and to the message of salvation has been adequately secured in the recent debate on the revised Sacramentary. What seems less clear is whether the need to show respect for fidelity to the assembly gathered here and now and to the style of prayer language that will serve their spiritual needs is receiving equal regard. Several avenues of further study would seem helpful here. One such effort would draw on the studies being done on orality; another would draw from performance disciplines such as reader's theater and from studies of human hearing, imagination, and how language and narrative engage the hearer.

Dwell for a moment on the study of orality.[24] Those who work in the field of humanities and anthropology tell us that text is an "inscribing medium," while utterance/speech is an "incorporating medium." For written prayer texts to be effective, they have to ap-

23. H. Belloc, *On Translating*, rpt. in J. E. Dineen, ed., *Selected Essays by Hilaire Belloc* (Philadelphia: Lippincott, 1936) 310–11.

24. The following two paragraphs are excerpted with slight revisions from my "Liturgical Translation: Some Reflections," an as-yet-unpublished talk given at an NCCB Forum on Translation in November 1998.

proximate speech/utterance. The more they do, the easier it is for a presider to lift them off the page and bring them to life for the assembly. Walter Ong has studied the difference between what he calls "primary oral cultures" and "literate cultures."[25] Oral cultures know nothing of writing or of reducing words to sign residues which can be stored and retrieved later; words are always spoken, sounded, power-laden. Think of the Hebrew understanding of God's word, *dabar*. Word not only says, it does what it says, it is event. In contrast to literate cultures, oral cultures show a predilection for a different style of speech. The contrasts noted by Ong and others who study orality include the following:

- for understanding and retention, oral style relies on rhythmic, balanced patterns, on repetition and antithesis, on alliteration and assonance; literate style relies on the ability to go back and re-read the inscribed text;
- oral style prefers to join ideas with conjunctions; literate style opts for subordinate clauses;
- oral style uses parallels, contrasts, epithets to keep things related; literate style separates things and analyzes them;
- oral style seeks redundance and is richly layered; literate style avoids redundance and is more spare;
- oral style speaks concretely of actual situations; literate style favors abstraction.

According to anthropologists, the words of ritual function more in the way speech does in oral cultures. This also serves the corporate purposes of ritual, for oral/aural language has a characteristic capacity to hold a group together (literally spellbound) and to facilitate remembrance and reiteration. Understanding orality is essential to understanding ritual performance and the work of crafting texts for it. Such study ought to be high on the agenda of those engaged in the work of preparing and reviewing liturgical translations.

Another kind of question follows from these few comments on orality. Has our liturgical language, like our worship space, become too plain and unadorned to feed the sacramental imagination of the faithful? Do teenagers have it right when they say "Boring!"? Might not the language of the liturgical prayer be served better by the characteristics of orality than of literacy? The Roman Rite in its fifth-century

25. W. Ong, *Orality and Literacy: The Technologizing of the Word* (New York: Methuen, 1982) esp. ch. 3: "Some Psychodynamics of Orality."

incarnation is said to be characterized by "noble simplicity" and this was put forward in Vatican II as the ideal for the liturgical renewal (see SC 34).[26] The liturgical renewal has taken this ideal quite seriously both in unadorned architecture and in a spare style of English. Nevertheless, other periods in the history of the Latin Rite and other historical Christian rites suggest that in other contexts liturgy thrives on repetition, formulaic phrases easily remembered, redundancy, concreteness, and life-relatedness in the language of prayer. Though the dominant North American culture cannot be said to retain a heavy residue of orality, the experience of many in our assemblies suggests that orality has much to offer in making prayers memorable and effective. The cultures of the British Isles, in contrast to the dominant culture in this country, still show the influence of orality. In particular, the Irish love of the graphic, vivid language of poetry, ballad, and song and the British love of the elegant flow of language have much to offer to balance our North American sense of blunt directness.[27] The great poetic and dramatic works of the Elizabethan period were written in an age when 90 percent of the people or more are said to have been functionally illiterate. The works of Shakespeare, Milton, and Dryden, the King James Bible, and Cranmer's Book of Common Prayer were all crafted to be heard. They are still effective benchmarks for spoken language today, not in their now dated vocabulary and archaic idioms, but in their patterns of speech stresses, assonance, alliteration, and rhythmic flow. Would this not be a worthwhile area to explore in the future if liturgical translations are to bring the riches of the English cultural heritage to the implanting of God's reign in our midst?[28]

26. See M. Wedig, *The Hermeneutics of Religious Visual Art in l'Art Sacré 1945–1954 in the Context of Aesthetic Modernity* (CUA doctoral dissertation, 1995) 117–25. Wedig discusses the influence of the French Dominicans in establishing the current widespread adoption of a nonrepresentational liturgical aesthetic. This aesthetic matches the ideal of the "noble simplicity" of the Roman liturgy as formulated by Edmund Bishop. See also Wedig's article forthcoming in *U.S. Catholic Historian*.

27. Perhaps the shining example in U.S. history showing that it is possible to combine the American penchant for what is now called "plain-speak" with the qualities of orality is Abraham Lincoln's Gettysburg Address. See G. Wills, *Lincoln at Gettysburg: The Words That Remade America* (New York: Simon & Schuster Touchstone Book, 1992) esp. 148–75.

28. See Vatican II, *Ad gentes* 22. In this context, it is interesting to note what Pope Gregory the Great wrote to Augustine of Canterbury in 599/600, as

Third and finally, behind ICEL's working principles one can detect a growing realization that translation is the first and most basic step in the inculturation of the liturgy; to adopt the living language of the people, history tells us, is to "open the door wide to inculturation."[29] Why is that so? The recent Roman instruction on inculturation puts it this way. The living language of a people *(sermo vivus)* is a preeminent means *(praecipuum instrumentum)* of communication among them.[30] Language lies at the very heart of a culture. The missionary endeavors of the Church have been quick to recognize and act on this.

"The missionary tradition of the Church has always sought to evangelize people in their own language. . . . And this is right, as it is by the mother language, which conveys the mentality and the culture of a people, that one can reach the soul, mold it in the Christian spirit and allow [it] to share more deeply in the prayer of the church."[31]

Inculturation, then, is a basic premise of liturgical translation. Anscar Chupungco, rightly noted for his work in this area, has written:

"In order that the assembly will grasp the full meaning of what is communicated, it is necessary that the content be expressed in the values, traditions, and linguistic patterns proper to the assembly. This vesture is the cultural form with which the doctrinal content is

---

recorded in Bede's *History of the English Church and People*, Book I:27, trans. Leo Shirley-Price (New York: Dorset Press, revised 1968) 73. See also *Select Epistles of Gregory the Great*, Book XI, Ep. LXIV, ad Q. 3, in *A Selection of Nicene and Post-Nicene Fathers of the Christian Church*, trans. J Barmby, 2nd series (Grand Rapids: Eerdmans, 1956) 13:75. In an unpublished, somewhat freer translation by Nathan Mitchell, the letter reads: "You know, brother, the custom of the Roman Church in which you were brought up; cherish it lovingly. But as far as I am concerned, if you've discovered something more pleasing to almighty God—in the Roman or the Gallican or any other church—choose carefully, gathering the best customs from many different churches, and arrange them for use in the church of the English, which is still a newcomer to the faith. For we should love things not because of the places where they're found, but because of the goodness they contain. Choose, therefore, those elements that are reverent *(pia)*, devout *(religiosa)*, and orthodox *(recta)*, and gathering them all into a dish (as it were), place it on the table of the English as their customary diet."

29. Chupungco, "The Cultural and Domestic Tradition," 25.

30. Congregation for Divine Worship and the Discipline of the Sacraments, *Instruction IV: Inculturation and the Roman Liturgy*, 39. The English translation of this document can be found in *Origins* 23 (43) (April 14, 1994) 746–56.

31. Ibid., 28.

expressed. It is through the form that the content is effectively communicated to the audience or assembly."[32]

We can begin to understand, then, why Chupungco calls liturgical translation such a "delicate and complex matter." What lies at the heart of the matter is not the substitution of English words for Latin ones, but the incarnation of the liturgy in our world. The 1969 *Instruction* clearly understands the inner logic of the Vatican II decision to return to the vernacular in liturgy. The initial translation of liturgical texts and their subsequent revision in the light of pastoral experience (1) are only the first two steps in the process. The *Instruction* envisions a further step when it concludes:

"Texts translated from another language are clearly not sufficient for the celebration of a fully renewed liturgy. The creation of new texts will be necessary. But translation of texts transmitted through the tradition of the Church is the best school and discipline for the creation of new texts . . ." (43).

The creation of new texts cannot but lead us more deeply into the full liturgical inculturation for which translation is already schooling us. For that next step to take place we will need to rely on that same Spirit who guided the Church when the Latin Liturgy was taking shape. We will also need to seek the scholarly wisdom and good pastoral services of those like Anscar Chupungco who are skilled in the theory and practice of inculturation.

---

32. Chupungco, "The Translation of Liturgical Texts," 388–89. See also his related discussion of inculturation as the fourth premise of liturgical translation, ibid., 393–95.

Burkhard Neunheuser, O.S.B.

Roman Genius Revisited*

"The Genius of the Roman Rite" is the text of a lecture given by Edmund Bishop on May 8, 1899, at Archbishop's House, Westminster, to an audience who, although generally interested in liturgical questions, were not liturgical scholars. This explains why Bishop, himself an extremely competent scholar, well known especially for his detailed studies, at first did not want the paper to appear in any periodical. He only allowed publication in an ordinary weekly magazine, the *Weekly Register*, in the same month in which the paper was delivered. Yet this little paper was to be published again and again throughout the following century. In fact, it is probably the reason for Bishop's fame, since his strictly academic works are now almost forgotten or remembered by only a small circle of scholars.

In my contribution to this *Festschrift* in honor of Fr. Anscar Chupungco, O.S.B., I would like first to give a brief publication history of the essay, and then to examine his conclusions by way of a rereading in light of the contemporary situation of the liturgical reform following the Second Vatican Council.

THE ESSAY AND ITS PUBLICATION HISTORY
This first section offers a summary of publications of this essay in the century following its first appearance. On May 8, 1899, the paper was first read at a meeting of the *Historical Research Society*, at Archbishop's House, Westminster. Later in the month it was published (in three parts) in the *Weekly Register*. A second edition appeared three years

* This essay was translated from German by Christian Göbel.

later under the auspices of P. E. Robinson, London. The paper was again reprinted in 1904 in V. Staley's *Essays on Ceremonial*, London. The most famous edition of this publication appeared in 1918: *Liturgica Historica. Papers on the Liturgy and Religious Life of the Western Church* (Oxford: Clarendon Press) 1–19. This book of 501 pages was edited by Bishop himself, but only published after his death on February 19, 1917, "leaving still unfinished the proofsheets of this book" (xi).

A number of further editions were published after Bishop's death. In 1919 André Wilmart, O.S.B., presented a French translation in *La Vie et Les Arts Liturgiques ("en trois morceaux")*: Février, Mai, Juin. Three years later in 1920 the text was reprinted in book form under the title *Le génie du Rite Romain* (Paris: Librairie de l'Art Catholique, 1921). The text follows a "preface" which in turn is followed by notes and a detailed index.

In 1931/32, Bishop's classic was translated into German by Dr. Johannes Pinsk of Berlin, and published in *Liturgische Zeitschrift* in the journal which he edited under the title "Der Geist des Römischen Ritus"; an introduction and commentary were included.

More recently, in 1996, a new edition of the English text edited by Cuthbert Johnson and Anthony Ward appeared in *Ephemerides Liturgicae* 110 (1996) 428–42. Then in 1997, a new edition of the French text was published in *Notitiae* 34 (1997) 237–62.

EVALUATIONS AND IMPORTANT REFERENCES
The work of John Wickham Legge, a scholar who played an important role in the foundation of the Henry Bradshaw Society, is remarkable.[1] Legge, a close friend of Bishop's because of their shared liturgical views, immediately recognized Bishop's solid view in his essay "The Genius . . ." He persisted in asking for a new edition of the essay, ignoring all doubts on the part of the author. In 1902 he was able to publish the second edition at P. E. Robinson's as mentioned above.[2] Legge did even more, however. He succeeded in his

---

1. Cf. the presentation of Anthony Ward and Cuthbert Johnson, "The Henry Bradshaw Society: Its Birth and First Decade," *Ephemerides Liturgicae* 104 (1990) 187–200, esp. 191–95; there is a short summary of this article in *Notitiae* 34 (1997) 217–19.

2. Cf. Bishop's correspondence concerning this publication in Cuthbert Johnson, O.S.B., and Anthony Ward, S.M., "Edmund Bishop's 'The Genius of the Roman Rite': Its Context, Import and Promotion," *Ephemerides Liturgicae* 110 (1996) 401–44, esp. 411–17.

struggle to have Bishop's works accepted into the British Museum Library. According to the letters which attest to these efforts, there can be no doubt that "The Genius" belonged to this group of writings. He noted: "I have given them particular warning of the value of the 'Genius'. . . ."[3]

Between 1919 and 1920 André Wilmart gave an opinion of the work in his French edition "Le génie du Rite Romain."[4] The famous French liturgical scholar opens his preface to the work as follows: "This lecture with its felicitous title, probably the most stimulating description of the Roman Liturgy and Mass, and the most judicious insight into its history so far presented, was given by Edmund Bishop on May 8th, 1899." Wilmart goes on to state that Bishop offers the results of his own academic research in a popular form, and without presenting too many details.[5] Such a sensible judgment from such a competent scholar underlines the importance of Bishop's sketch, but equally demonstrates its limits—limits imposed by the absence of detailed analysis from the text. However, the accuracy of his basic ideas was proved by the academic research of subsequent decades.

In 1922 Odo Casel discussed Bishop's basic ideas in his essay "Mysterium und Martyrium in den römischen Sakramentarien."[6] Casel attempted to demonstrate, using examples from the Roman Sacramentaries, that even the sober Roman liturgy is a vivid celebration of the Christian mysteries,[7] and in so doing, he refers explicitly to Bishop's *The Genius of the Roman Rite*, and its French translation by

3. Cited from a letter of May 23, 1903; ibid., 418.

4. Edmund Bishop, "Le génie du Rit Romain," Edition française annotée par Dom. André Wilmart, Bénédictin de St. Michel de Farnborough (Paris: Librairie de l'Art Catholique, 1921).

5. "Cette lecture, qui est probablement, sous un titre heureux, l'exposé le plus suggestif qu'on ait encore fait de la liturgie et de la messe romaine, et l'aperçu le plus judicieux qu'on ait présenté de leur histoire, fut donnée par E. Bishop . . . le 8 mai 1899" (7). . . . "La conférence offre, sous une forme populaire, un résumé des conclusions auxquelles l'auteur était dès lors arrivé et dont quelques unes furent ensuite présentées avec plus de détail dans des mémoires techniques . . ." (8).

6. JLw 2 (1922) 18–38.

7. "durch einige Beispiele aus den römischen Sakramentarien . . . erhärten, daß in der christlichen, ja auch in der sonst so nüchternen und zurückhaltenden römischen Liturgie das Wort von der Mysterienfeier durchaus lebendig ist."

Dom. Wilmart (cf. the first note of his text). He also quotes the last summary from Bishop's *Liturgica Historica* (1918) that "soberness and sense" are the "essentially Roman characteristics of the massbook." He also noted that this Roman style is free from all "that can be called sentiment and effusiveness or imagination or mystery." Casel, although in general agreement with Bishop, repeats this reservation even more distinctly at the conclusion of his essay, writing: "To Edmund Bishop's somehow one-sided description of the Roman Rite, a description which stresses only its soberness and sense, we may add the sense of mystical depth through clear arrangement and monumental greatness."[8]

Although the well-known scholar Hieronymus Engberding, O.S.B., monk of Gerleve Abbey in Germany, makes only passing references to Bishop, he nevertheless makes a statement which demonstrates his profound appreciation of Bishop's essay. At the beginning of his essay *"Die spanischwestgotische Liturgie. Eine Einführung in ihr Wesen und ihren Geist,"*[9] he states that he wants to give an introduction which does not aim to present as much detail as possible, but rather "following the example of the great Edmund Bishop, who, in his lecture 'The Genius of the Roman Rite' wanted to give his audience a profound knowledge of the Roman Rite, but a knowledge which any educated person would want to have without having to be a scholar."[10]

It was these words which induced Johannes Pinsk, the famous pioneer of the liturgical movement in Germany, "to present an introduction to the Roman Rite in a similarly concentrated form"[11] in the same periodical, the *Liturgische Zeitschrift,* of which he was the editor. Pinsk continues, "To this end, I refer to the work of the famous Eng-

8. "Jedenfalls dürfen wir die etwas einseitige Charakteristik des römischen Ritus durch E. Bishop, der an ihm nur seine Nüchternheit und Verständigkeit hervorzuheben wußte, dahin ergänzen, daß ihm mystiche Tiefe bei klar geprägten und monumentale Größe nicht abgeht" (38).

9. "The Spanish Visigothic Liturgy: An Introduction to Its Practices and Spirit," *Liturgische Zeitschrift* 4 (1931/32) 156; cf. also 155–66, 241–49.

10. ". . . sondern wir tun dies im Geiste des großen Edmund Bishop, der mit seinem Vortrag 'The Genius of the Roman Rite' seinen Hörern eine wirkliche Kenntnis des römischen Ritus vermitteln wollte, eine solche Kenntnis, wie sie angestrebt werden kann von einem Gebildeten, der kein Fachmann ist, der aber einige allgemeine Kentnisse bezüglich seines Wesens zu besitzen wünscht" (156).

11. "in ähnlich konzentrierter Form auch für den Römischen Ritus eine Einführung zu geben."

lish liturgical scholar, Edmund Bishop, already mentioned by P. Engberding,"[12] and thus introduces the German translation which has been considered definitive since then, under the title *"Der Geist des Römischen Ritus."*[13] He presents not only Bishop's text, but also his own helpful annotations for German readers, and I would like to cite one of these: a comment which is important in its historical context, and is worth considering in the context of our own postconciliar times. Pinsk writes, "It is significant that sometimes today, one finds efforts being made to integrate pedagogical and catechetical elements into the liturgy, completely in contrast to the thought of Edmund Bishop, who understands the sense of the liturgy correctly. Imagine what this would mean for the Mass! Liturgy is not catechizing or sermonizing. These are, of course, important, but they must precede or follow the Liturgy."[14]

In 1959 Nigel Abercrombie published an extensive biography, *The Life and Work of Edmund Bishop.*[15] David Knowles rightly notes in his preface that when Edmund Bishop died in 1917 at the age of seventy, "his name was virtually unknown, save to a couple of dozen scholars scattered over four or five countries of Europe" which was just approaching the bitterest period of the First World War.

Despite this, Balthasar Fischer, writing in the restored journal *Lexikon für Theologie und Kirche,*[16] calls him "an important English historian of the Liturgy" and an "initiator of Benedictine liturgical research." He also remarks that among all Bishop's various works, it was "The Genius of the Roman Rite" which was the best known.

---

12. "Zu diesem Zweck greife ich auf das Werk des berühmten englischen Liturgikers Edmund Bishop zurück, auf das schon P. Engberding hingewiesen hatte."

13. *Liturgische Zeitschrift* 4, 395–417.

14. "Es ist bezeichnend daß auch heute wieder ganz im Gegensatz zu der Auffassung E. Bishop, der den Sinn der Liturgie richtig versteht, von manchen Kreisen pädagogisch-katechetische Zusätze und Einschaltungen in die liturgischen Formeln gemacht werden. . . . Man stelle sich vor, was das für die Messe bedeuten würde! Liturgische Funktionen können nicht zu Katechismusstunden oder belehrenden Predigten gemacht werden. Diese sind nötig, müssen aber vorhergehen oder folgen." Ibid., 401.

15. N. Abercrombie, *The Life and Work of Edmund Bishop* (London: Longmans, 1959). This is the best biography available, and contains a preface by David Knowles (xi–xv), ten chapters (3–491), a bibliography (492–508), an appendix (509–20), and an index (521–39).

16. *LThK* (1994:2) 508.

The biography gives a solid summary of Bishop's rich and manifold life. Although Bishop never succeeded in his attempt to become a monk at Downside Abbey, he never lost contact with Benedictine life. He played an important part in the burgeoning development of Benedictine life in England, and in the development of the modern English Benedictine Congregation, participating in vivid exchanges with the abbeys Downside, Beuron, Maredsous, and Solesmes. The growth of a flourishing Catholic life in England was encouraged by the abolition of restrictive legislation in the mid-Victorian period, but the period was also characterized by the problems surrounding the Church at the time of the First Vatican Council. Despite these problems, Bishop remained tireless in stimulating and continuing discussion with contemporary scholars, including Aidan Gasquet, O.S.B., who later became a cardinal.

Finally, in line with these generally positive assessments, I must admit that I too adopted Bishop's views in my lectures at the Pontifical Liturgical Institute "De ingenio ritus Romani"—first given in Latin (from 1963–70): *Historia Liturgica per epocas culturales II* (1968),[17] and then, from 1970, in Italian: *Storia della Liturgia attraverso le epoche culturali* (1977).[18] In presenting the history of the adaptation of the original Roman Liturgy in the medieval Franco-Germanic churches, I wanted to demonstrate that the "genius" (i.e., the essential characteristic features) of the classical Roman Liturgy had never been lost. On the contrary, even after the multiple additions from different cultures resulting in the *liturgia Romano-Germanica, secundum usum Romanae Curiae,* and the subsequent changes at Trent, the classical form was preserved, and was then "rediscovered" and "renewed" in the work of Vatican II. In fact, I took the title of the central part of my lectures "De ingenio" from Bishop's essay, which I quoted explicitly at the beginning of the short biography appended to the text; alongside this, I presented Bishop's basic ideas in detail in the Latin edition more briefly in the Italian version. I summarized these ideas in the following way: "formal elements" are to be translated "in their simplicity—precise, sober, short, free of verbosity and undue sentimentality; their arrangement clear and lucid; their greatness both sacred and—at the

17. Manuscript edition. Pars II (Rome: Pontifical Athenaeum S. Anselmi de Urbe, 1968) 19–23.
18. Rome: Edizioni Liturgiche, 1977, 64–66. The relevant sections are "Il genio di questa Liturgia Romana (pura): Gli elementi formali: Gli elementi teologici."

same time—human, both spiritual and of great literary value."[19] To emphasize the above, I quoted the comment of Theodore Klauser, who, although generally in agreement with Bishop, is quite independent. He calls the Roman liturgy "one of the great classical creations of Mankind," without "closing his eyes to some of its obvious weak spots."[20] I completed the analysis with an insistence on the theological elements which were constitutive for the "genius" of the entire Roman liturgy in the "classical" period.[21] By way of example, I mentioned the constant direction of prayer *ad Patrem, per Christum, in Spiritu Sancto;* the realization of a *pietas eucharistica;* the importance of the fact that it is always a local community of worshipers that celebrates Sunday; and finally that it is the Church "in qua semper apostolicae cathedrae viguit principatus."[22]

Recently, Cuthbert Johnson, O.S.B., and Anthony Ward, S.M., have given a solid presentation and evaluation of the life and work of Edmund Bishop, with special emphasis on the essay of 1899, "The Genius of the Roman Rite." Their work first appeared in an English edition, *The Genius of the Roman Rite: Its Context, Import and Promotion,*[23] and soon after in a French translation with the title *Un liturgist anglais, Edmund Bishop, l'auteur du Génie du Rit Romain.*[24] The editions complement each other with the English version presenting more detail, particularly in the presentation of Bishop's correspondence. Both are based on wide and exacting research, including references to the biography of Abercrombie. However, that both authors were staff members of the *Congregatio de Cultu Divino et Disciplina Sacramentorum* and that the French version appeared in the official bulletin of that congregation seems significant to me. Both versions give special emphasis to the "Genius"—including a special chapter, "The Episode of the Genius"[25] or "L'episode du Génie," and each

---

19. "la loro semplicità precisa, sobria, breve, non verbosa, poco sentimentale; la loro disposizione chiara e lucida; la grandezza sacra ed insieme umana, spirituale e di gran valore letterario."

20. Kleine Abendländische Liturgiegeschichte (Bonn, 1965) 41–44.

21. Cf. 20–23 in the Latin edition; 64–66 in the Italian version.

22. Augustine, *Ep.* 43.7.

23. Cf. n. 3. The 1918 edition of Bishop's text in English is presented on 428–42.

24. *Notitiae* 34 (1997) 212–64. The French translation by Dom Wilmart of Bishop's lecture is included in the article.

25. *Eph. Lit.* 110 (1996) 409–18

reaches its climax with a presentation of the text itself, the English version being that edited by Bishop himself for the volume *Liturgica Historica*. Both English and French versions thus give a wide and valuable insight into Bishop's life and work, and above all, into his most famous essay, "The Genius of the Roman Rite."

We must now ask what this influential essay has to say to us today. Bishop wanted to define "the particular native spirit animating and penetrating that rite (the Roman), which differentiates it from others, Gallican or Gothic, Greek or Oriental."[26]

However, we must be careful to note that the Roman Missal, at least in the form in which it existed in the second half of the nineteenth century, is a very varied document. This "Roman" book is not completely "Roman" in the sense that Bishop describes it. In fact, although its origins lie in the fourth and fifth centuries, its contents were variously modified in the course of subsequent centuries. Bishop compares the style of these supplementary texts to that of the old "Gallican and Spanish" (Mozarabic) books, while I would prefer to call it a Franco-Germanic style.[27] In contrast to these new influences the "genius" of the original Roman Liturgy is marked by "simplicity, practicality, a great sobriety and self-control, gravity and dignity." Bishop summarizes his characterization at the end of his essay in the following way, "in two or three words . . . those characteristics were essentially soberness and sense."[28]

Such comments must be understood in the context of the arguments between Roman Catholics and Anglicans in late nineteenth-century England. In fact, Bishop reveals that many of the elements of the Roman liturgy disliked by the Anglicans were not originally "Roman" at all—that is, they did not form part of the classical "Roman" Liturgy, but were Franco-Germanic accretions added to the "properly Roman" base over the centuries of the medieval period.[29]

26. *Liturgica Historica*, 2.

27. Cf. Bishop's own words, "This process was going on during the whole of the ninth century in France and Germany" (*Liturgica Historica*, 6).

28. In Wilmart's French translation "la sobriété et le bon sens"; in Pinsk's German version "Nüchternheit und gesunder Menschenverstand."

29. Cf. Abercrombie's judgment: "On reading the paper after the lapse of more than half a century, the impression received is of a just, quiet, authoritative appreciation of the inestimable contribution that the authentic liturgy of Rome has made. . . . What is considered most picturesque . . . all this came from elsewhere; from Rome (came) simplicity, practicality, gravity, absence of poetry" (277).

These ideas, put forward almost one hundred years ago, are still relevant when we consider the Second Vatican Council and the liturgical reforms initiated by it.

THE ESSAY "RE-VISITED" TODAY

It is now more than thirty years since the close of the Second Vatican Council, for which Bishop's ideas had great relevance, and we have to ask if we can still agree with the judgments of Bishop's short paper.

First, there can be no doubt today that the *Missale Romanum,* and the "Roman Rite" in general, are very complex structures. So much has been discovered by academic research done in the years subsequent to Bishop's death. The "Roman Rite" has developed over a period of some fifteen hundred years. The classical *liturgia romana* of the fourth and fifth centuries is not simply identical with the *liturgia secundum usum Romanae Curiae* of the thirteenth century, nor with the "Tridentine Liturgy" of the sixteenth and seventeenth centuries. Nor is it identical with our own contemporary liturgy which issues from the postconciliar liturgical reform. We must be clearly aware that not all of the "Roman" Liturgy of the last millennium is essentially Roman.

Thus we have to state that Bishop's characterization of the Roman Rite can only be held valid for the "native Roman Rite," as Bishop himself calls it; only this "is marked by simplicity, practicality, a great sobriety and self-control, gravity and dignity."[30]

Even though we now know that the historical development of the Roman Rite is more complicated than Bishop's "rapid review of that history"[31] could demonstrate, I would still like to follow his judgment here. Indeed, I believe that the original "classical" Roman Liturgy of the first centuries, the "native Roman Rite," has to be characterized as Bishop does it. The basic features can still be recognized, even through the modifications of later history, although Bishop's characterization remains most valid for the *orationes* of the old Roman Sacramentaries. For other elements, those essentially theological, the lectionaries, etc., I think we must search for other distinctive features.

Nonetheless, Bishop's appreciation of the "native Roman Rite" retains validity. In fact, it was adopted by the bishops and scholars, theological faculties and other authorities who, during the period of preparation before Vatican II, desired a reform of the existing

30. *Liturgica Historica,* 12.
31. Cf. *Liturgica Historica,* 13–18.

liturgy.[32] Having sufficiently outlined the main ideas of this lecture by Bishop a hundred years ago and its continuous influence throughout the following century, we must ask which of these ideas can still be considered important today.

First, there is Bishop's view, certainly correct, that the greatness of the original Roman Liturgy lies in its simplicity and sobriety, though it is never easy to determine the exact limits between the older, original, classical Roman Liturgy and its later supplements. I would like to express this in Bishop's own words: "As we view the character of the Roman as he revealed himself in the course of his long history, we feel that it was not in his soul that arose the idea of sackcloth and ashes, and the priests, the Lord's ministers, weeping between the porch and the altar. . . . But it is precisely in this simplicity, this gravity, this absence of poetry . . . that lies the value and the importance of the native Roman Rite for the history of public worship in western Europe."

Second, Bishop was correct in noting that this native Roman Liturgy, although retained as the heart of all later forms, was greatly modified. It is true that Charlemagne desired a close connection with

32. These consilia et vota have been published in Acta et Documenta Concilio Oec.Vat. II. apparando. Series I (Antepreparatorio). Vol. II: Consilia et vota episcoporum ac praelatorum. Pars I & II (1960); the following parts are about other continents: Vols. I and II, "Proposita et monita Congregationum Curiae Romanae"; Vol. IV, "Studia et vota Universitatem et Facultatem Ecclesiasticatum et Catholicarum."

From the variety of these imposingly large volumes, I would like to refer here to the "Consilia et vota episcopi Berlinensi" (i.e., Berlin): "Cardinal Doepfner," November 6, 1959 (Vol. II, pars I [1960] 577–93). After some general considerations he presents (586–91) an exact explanation of the "Desideria quaedam nostris regionibus gravissima," the Caeremoniale Episcoporum, the Pontificale, the Missale Romanum, the Breviarum Romanum, Rituale, SS. Eucharistai, Annus Liturgicus, and finally the "normae quaedam de S. Liturgia reformanda." I would simply like to quote the following from these: "1. S. Liturgia . . . ab omnibus participantibus sine nimis difficultate intelligi debest. Verba et caeremoniae claritate et perspicuitate quam maxima fulgeant. Actus praeparatorii et ornantes ne luxurientur . . . 2. Signa symbolica et verba et caeremoniae eo efficaciora sunt, quo minore indigent declaratione . . . 4. Repititiones vitentur secundum regulam: ne bis idem" (591).

This must be enough for our purposes. I think the example of the cardinal, who later played an important role among the Council Fathers, is significant. Of course not all of the many hundreds of vota asked for simplicity, sobriety, and clarity as he did; still, I consider this statement by the Cardinal Bishop of Berlin as quite symptomatic.

Rome, but as Bishop puts it, "he had also the ruler's instinct, and enough perhaps of the Frankish spirit to recognize that to many, perhaps, this pure Roman book must seem to be dry and jejune, or prove in practice a curb, too hard to be borne, on natures more florid, or more sensitive, or more rich. As a practical statesman he forthwith caused this Gregorian mass book to be accordingly enriched with a supplement of additions selected from the liturgical books already in use in France." Aside from the concrete realizations of these supplementary influences, Bishop found the essential: as we see even more clearly today, the "Roman" Liturgy forms the kernel of all subsequent forms of Catholic liturgy, that is the liturgy of the *Pontificale Romano-Germanicum*, the liturgy *secundum usum Romanae Curiae*, the *Missale Romanum* of Pius V. However, the developments of later times make us see that the genius of the old, original Roman Liturgy lies not only in its "soberness and sense," but also in the theological elements which underlie that Roman Liturgy. Actually, it was this fact among others which finally convinced the fathers of the Second Vatican Council to allow the reforms of *Sacrosanctum concilium* 38, but only under the condition "provided that the fundamental unity of the Roman Rite is preserved."[33]

What does this mean today? Some years ago, I published an article in *Ecclesia Orans,* the periodical of the Pontifical Liturgical Institute at Sant' Anselmo in Rome, trying to explain the sense of this restricting condition in some way.[34] The council wanted to allow the possibility of "legitimate variations and adaptations to meet the needs of different gatherings, areas and peoples . . . provided that the fundamental unity of the Roman Rite is preserved" (SC 38).[35] J. A. Jungmann, S.J., interpreted this principle as being "in favor of a unity in essential features, along with a vast differentiation in details."[36] Again, we must ask, what are the essential features *("das Wesentliche")* of the Roman Rite? In my article, I expressed it as follows: "Certainly, it is not the Latin language, nor the details of the Ordo Missae, nor the order of the Lectionary, the addition of a homily, the intercessions or other de-

33. "Servata substantiali unitate ritus romani," *Sacrosanctum concilium* 38.

34. "Servata substantiali unitate ritus romani," *Ecclesia Orans* 8 (1991) 77–95.

35. "legitimis varietatibus et aptationibus ad diversos coetos, regiones, populos . . . servata substantiali unitate ritus romani. . . ."

36. "zugunsten einer Einheit im Wesentlichen bei einer weitgehenden Differenzierung im einzelnen"—cf. his commentary on *Sacrosanctum concilium* (*LThK, Ergänzungsband, 1. Teil* [1966] 43ff.).

tails. It is something much more important and fundamental."[37] In interpreting what is essential, I pointed to the *Instructio "Inter Oecumenici"* of 26 September 1964, which states that it was not the intention of the liturgical reform simply to change the forms and texts, but to implement a pastoral practice the decisive power of *which "in eo posita est ut Mysterium Paschale vivendo exprimatur."*[38]

However, we cannot concern ourselves solely with these characteristics of the first elements and heart of the Roman Liturgy in the way that Bishop saw them as a strict scholar of the liturgy. The essence of classical Roman Liturgy also includes its proper theological elements, a fact only revealed by later academic research, in particular that of the famous pioneers of the liturgical movement at the beginning of the twentieth century, which led directly to the reforms of the Second Vatican Council and the postconciliar realizations of its work. These theological elements are as follows: the celebration of the liturgy is an *"actio sacra,"* the *"opus Christi sacerdotis eiusque corporis quod est Ecclesia, actio sacra praecellenter"* (SC 7), the *"culmen . . . et . . . fons . . ."* (SC 10). All this, I think, as described by the Second Vatican Council, equally forms part of the genius of the Roman Liturgy. It, too, was preserved more or less in its original state as the heart of the liturgy, even throughout periods of modification, and was rediscovered and especially stressed in the postconciliar reforms. Concretely, I am referring to the theocentric and christocentric orientation of worship: *ad Patrem per Christum Dominum in Spiritu Sancto.*[39] The *anamnesis* of the *"Mysterium Christi"* is celebrated in an orderly fashion throughout the Liturgical Year. Central to it is the feast of Easter, and its weekly celebration on Sunday, the *Dies Dominica.* Although the memory of the saints also plays an important part in the Liturgical Year, still the feasts of Christ always remain more important. The heart of all these different kinds of worship is the Eucharist, the memorial of the death and resurrection of Christ, fulfilled in the Communion-offering, naturally under both species. All this is surrounded by the daily celebra-

37. "Es ist jedenfalls niche die lateinische Sprache, es sind auch nicht die Einzelheiten im Ordo Missae, wie Lesordnung, Praxis der Homilie, der Forbitten and andere Details. Es ist etwas bedeutend Wesentlicheres," *Ecclesia Orans* 8 (1991) 90.

38. See n. 3 (EDIL n. 203) and n. 6 (EDIL n. 204) of the *Instructio.*

39. Cf. J. A. Jungmann, *Die Stellung Christi im liturgischen Gebet* (Münster i.W.: LWF, 1962). Though the first edition of this book was published more than seventy years ago (1923), its presentation of this problem is still valid.

tion of the Liturgy of the Hours, worthily prayed *"in veritate temporis."*[40]

Admiring the particular spirit of the Roman Liturgy, we should do everything we can to preserve it, agreeing to the possibility offered by the council to "save the essential unity along with a vast differentiation in details" as Jungmann puts it. This differentiation means reorganizing the liturgy in the new liturgical languages, and adapting it to the temperament and character of the new cultures into which the Roman Liturgy is transmitted, always *"servate substantiali unitate ritus romani."* Such adaptations are not only to be made for the sake of the new churches in the third world, but also for our churches in Western Europe and North America. We too must adapt ourselves to the characteristic features of the Roman Liturgy, both the native genius as described by Bishop and also the theological elements which I have added. Finally, we have to consider that the goal of the whole liturgical reform of the council is that *actio pastoralis,* of which the *"vis in eo posita est, ut Mysterium Paschale vivendo exprimatur,"* as the already-quoted Instructio *"Inter Oecumenici"* emphasizes.[41]

Edmund Bishop knew all about these contexts and connotations, and he mentioned many of them in his courageous lecture, "The Genius of the Roman Rite." Certainly, he could not say everything at that time and we must add something today. Still, his words can be taken as prophetic. The preservation of the spiritual essence of the Roman Rite, even with the necessary adaptations resulting from contact with new peoples and cultures, is not merely a historical fact; it must remain the goal of the liturgy of our times. Bishop appeals to us "to save the important intellectual heritage of the Roman liturgy of the first two millennia." This heritage is not one novelty or another such as an African dance, an Asian way of meditation, or Latin-American sociopolitical ideas. It is the particular spirit which was characterized by Bishop as the "Genius of the Roman Rite" at the beginning of this, the twentieth century. By means of the reform of the essential basic structures of the Roman Liturgy, the Western Church has been able to transmit the heritage of its long history to the young

40. Cf. my various attempts to explain the totality of the genius of the classical Roman Liturgy, e.g., *Storia della Liturgia* (1977) 64–74; *ALw* 30 (1988) 271–74; *Ecclesia Orans* 8 (1991) 89–93.

41. On the interpretation of these postulates of the postconciliar liturgical reform, see my article in the *Festschrift* in honor of Fr. A. Nocent, *Traditio et Progressio* (Rome: Studia Anselmiana 95, 1988) 375–89.

churches of Asia, Latin America, and Africa, so that they too may both preserve it and express it in the various ways of their own cultures. This is the teaching of the Second Vatican Council; it is also our hope.[42]

42. "das entscheidende geistige Erbgut der römischen Liturgie der ersten zwei Jahrtausende zu bewahren . . . . Es geht nicht um die eine oder andere Neuheit, etwa ein afrikanisches Tanzen oder fernöstliche Meditationsweisen oder lateinamerikanische sozialpolitische Ausrichtungen. Es geht um das Eigentliche, das zu Anfang unseres (des 20.) Jahrhunderts E. Bishop andeutete, als er vom 'Genius of the Roman Rite' sprach . . . Die abendländische Kirche hat in dieser Erneuerung der wesentlichen Grundstrukturen römischer Liturgie das Erbe ihrer zweitausendjährigen Geschichte den jungen Völkern Asiens, Lateinamerikas und Afrikas überliefert, auf daß sie es bewahren und doch in den Formen ihrer Kulturen zum Ausdruck bringen. Solches ist der Auftrag des Zweiten Vatikanischen Konzils, und es ist unsere Hoffnung." Cf. my essay "Ein Vierteljahrhundert Liturgiereform," *ALw* 30 (1998) 272–73.

Keith F. Pecklers, S.J.

The Liturgical Assembly at the Threshold of the Millennium: A North American Perspective

This essay proposes to do two things. First, the role of the liturgical assembly will be traced historically, examining the principal developments and significant turning points, culminating with the Second Vatican Council's restoration of a participative liturgy for the whole Church. Second, acknowledging that the liturgical assembly of the year 2000 looks somewhat different from the time of the 1960s, the sociological dimensions of the contemporary liturgical assembly will be examined.

THE MYSTICAL BODY OF CHRIST GATHERED TOGETHER

In the Pauline tradition, there was an intrinsic union between the liturgical assembly and that which they were commissioned to celebrate by virtue of their common baptism. In other words, it was the body of Christ, the *ekklesia*, that celebrated the body of Christ, the Eucharist.[1]

Reflecting on that same tradition four centuries later, Augustine, bishop of Hippo, preached to the newly baptized: "You are the body and the members of Christ; it is your own mystery you receive. It is to what you are that you reply 'Amen.' . . . Be a member of the body of Christ and let your 'Amen' be true."[2]

It was such an intrinsic union between the liturgical assembly and the Eucharist that enabled Christians to see a life in common, radically transformed because of their liturgical participation, even despite

1. Cf. 1 Corinthians 10:17.
2. Sermon 272.

49

their differences and the challenges they faced. Liturgical participation demanded *caritas,* not only for the other members of that same assembly, but even more for the weaker members who stood on the fringe of that society.

Unlike caste systems and social differences separating rich and poor in the secular world, the liturgical assembly offered no special treatment for the privileged elite since Christian initiation was the great equalizer. When a wealthy or prominent citizen entered the assembly, the presiding bishop was to do nothing, lest he be seen as catering to the elite. If, however, a poor person entered that same assembly, everything changed. We read in the third-century Syrian document *Didascalia Apostolorum* that the bishop was to get up from his seat to find room for that destitute newcomer even if it meant giving up the presider's bench and sitting himself on the floor.[3]

Lest we be too quick to canonize that golden age of liturgical patrimony, we can be sure that, like all social groupings, there were rough edges and tensions in the community even when it gathered together for worship. Then as now, this Mystical Body of Christ gathered in worship was a community of graced sinners. Indeed, as historian Peter Brown notes: "The Catholic Church was a united community precisely because it was a community of sinners."[4]

THE WESTERN MIDDLE AGES AND THE FRAGMENTATION BETWEEN COMMUNITY AND SYMBOL

A symbolic image of the Eucharist gradually gave way to an instrumental view, turning the Eucharist into an object to be adored rather than an action to be celebrated. This had obvious implications for the liturgical assembly, widening the gap between that "community of sinners" and the sacred elements of the Body and Blood of Christ lying on the altar.[5] This shift in theological understanding grew in the Middle Ages and provided the underpinnings for a clericalized liturgy that left the liturgical assembly largely passive.

The one altar and the one Eucharist celebrated together by the one body of Christ was replaced with many altars and many Eucharists. Private Masses abounded, especially in monasteries and residences

3. *Didascalia Apostolorum* 12 (2.57).
4. Peter Brown, *The Rise of Western Christendom: Triumph and Diversity* A.D. *200–1000* (Oxford: Blackwell Publishers, 1997) 51.
5. See Bernard Cooke, *The Distancing of God: The Ambiguity of Symbol in History and Theology* (Minneapolis: Fortress Press, 1990).

of priests. The theological doctrine of the "fruits of the Mass" assisted an understanding of the Eucharist where the priest alone celebrated Mass for the community or for some particular intention, and the presence of the assembly was no longer deemed necessary. By the late Middle Ages some clerics considered the presence of an assembly a distraction to the *Opus Dei* that the Church had commissioned them to do. When they were present, lay women and men "heard Mass" often without receiving the Eucharist, occupying themselves with devotions and adoring the sacrament after the consecration and at benediction.

THE COUNCIL OF TRENT AND THE ROLE OF THE LITURGICAL ASSEMBLY IN THE MISSAL OF PIUS V (1570)

Influenced by his Augustinian heritage and grounded in the doctrine of the priesthood of all believers, Martin Luther led his reform with a strong call for a more participative liturgy through use of the vernacular, congregational singing, Communion from the chalice, and liturgical preaching.

The Council of Trent, while attempting to respond to reformers like Luther, Calvin, and Zwingli, did, in fact, discuss the possibility of increased liturgical participation, e.g., through use of the vernacular. In the end, however, the bishops of the council decided that such changes were pastorally inopportune, and the result was a centralized liturgy that made the private Mass rubrically normative for all liturgical celebrations, even those with the presence of an assembly.

The twenty-second session of the Council of Trent encouraged Catholics to attend Mass on Sundays and feast days. Beyond that exhortation, we find no reference to the liturgical assembly. Likewise, in the rubrics of the 1570 Missal of Pius V, references to the liturgical assembly were eliminated since, as an exclusively clerical action, there would be no need for such instructions.[6] As Burkhard Neunheuser notes: "any reference to the faithful here is accidental; their presence is not required. It is sometimes presupposed, but it always remains a passive presence." He continues:

"The only forms of a slightly more active participation were: to stand during the gospel, to adore the eucharistic elements after the

6. See Burkhard Neunheuser, "The Relation of Priest and Faithful in the Liturgies of Pius V and Paul VI," *Roles in the Liturgical Assembly*, trans. Matthew J. Connell (New York: Pueblo Publishing Co., 1981) 207–19.

consecration (but this adoration did not properly belong to the eucharistic celebration as such!), and—rather rarely—to receive communion (from hosts consecrated at that same Mass)."[7]

THE LITURGICAL MOVEMENT PAVES THE WAY

The liturgical reforms of the Second Vatican Council were able to take place because of the pioneering work done on both sides of the Atlantic in the first half of the twentieth century, led by the German Benedictine monastery of Maria Laach with their first *missa recitata* (or dialogue Mass, inviting the assembly's responses with the help of animators and with the presider facing the people) on the sixth of August 1921. These dialogue Masses grew increasingly common throughout Europe and North America as a viable means of fostering liturgical participation. Moreover, experiments with use of the vernacular further assisted such efforts.[8]

While accepting the fundamental unity of the Mystical Body of Christ, liturgical pioneers like Martin Hellriegel of St. Louis, Missouri, called liturgical assemblies to glory in their diversity, challenging the melting pot theory where all is blended into sameness while favoring the image of a mosaic where every tessera is precious and necessary for the successful completion of the piece.[9] In France, beginning in 1949, liturgical scholars like Aimé-George Martimort, Pierre Jounel, Thierry Maertens, and others labored to recover the fundamental identity and theological significance of the liturgical assembly.[10]

Those efforts of the liturgical movement, assisted by encyclicals like *Mediator Dei,* paved the way for a conciliar liturgy that would affirm the corporate nature of Christian worship and exhort the assembly to take its ministry seriously, faithful to its own baptismal priesthood. The Second Vatican Council's first major document, *Sacrosanctum concilium,* the Constitution on the Sacred Liturgy, awakened the liturgical assembly to its proper role within Christian worship, recapturing its identity as the Mystical Body of Christ:

7. Ibid., 211.

8. See Keith F. Pecklers, *The Unread Vision: The Liturgical Movement in the United States of America, 1926–1955* (Collegeville: The Liturgical Press, 1998) 55–59.

9. Ibid., 34.

10. See Catherine Vincie, "The Liturgical Assembly: Review and Reassessment," *Worship* 67 (1993) 123–44.

"The Church earnestly desires that all the faithful be led to that full, conscious, and active participation in liturgical celebrations called for by the very nature of the liturgy. Such participation by the Christian people as 'a chosen race, a royal priesthood, a holy nation, God's own people' (1 Pt 2:9; see 2:4-5) is their right and duty by reason of their baptism."[11]

The document continues:

"Christ's faithful, when present at this mystery of faith, should not be there as strangers or silent spectators. On the contrary . . . they should take part in the sacred action, conscious of what they are doing, with devotion and full collaboration."[12]

This was a radical shift in the assembly's self-identity. It reclaimed baptism rather than ordination as the common denominator for all Christian ministry—and emphasized a diversity of gifts within the liturgical assembly which symbolize and represent the diversity of talents and gifts within the one body of Christ. This reclaiming of the assembly's self-identity was radical not because it was a flippant innovation with no origins in Church tradition, but precisely because it returned to that early Church vision of the liturgical assembly convoked by God and actively celebrating its identity as primary minister of the liturgy itself.

THE LITURGICAL ASSEMBLY IN THE LITURGY OF VATICAN II

The *General Instruction on the Roman Missal* (1969) further describes the ministry of the assembly as People of God:

"In the celebration of Mass the faithful are a holy people, a people God has made his own, a royal priesthood: they give thanks to the Father and offer the victim not only through the hands of the priest but also together with him and learn to offer themselves. They should endeavor to make this clear by their deep sense of reverence for God and their charity toward all who share with them in the celebration.

"They therefore are to shun any appearance of individualism or division, keeping before their mind that they have one Father in heaven and therefore are all brothers and sisters to each other.

---

11. *Sacrosanctum concilium* 14.
12. *Sacrosanctum concilium* 48.

"They should become one body, whether by hearing the word of God, or joining in prayers and song, or above all by offering the sacrifice together and sharing together in the Lord's table."[13]

Thus, in the conciliar liturgy, the assembly has again become the primary symbol of the liturgy: the subject rather than the object of liturgical action, providing the proper context for all liturgical ministry. Presiders and musicians, readers, servers, and ministers of hospitality, deacons and eucharistic ministers, are first and foremost members of the assembly and their servant-role only makes sense in relationship to the assembly.

That vision of the assembly as subject of the liturgical action was affirmed in 1978 when the U.S. Bishops' Committee on the Liturgy issued the document "Art and Environment in Catholic Worship": "Among the symbols with which the liturgy deals, none is more important than the assembly of believers."[14] Several years later, in 1982, the Bishops' Committee on Priestly Life and Ministry spoke of the assembly as the starting point for the homily, rather than the preacher or the homily itself. The document continues: "The church, therefore, is first and foremost a gathering of those whom the Lord has called into a covenant of peace with himself. In this gathering, as in every other, offices and ministries are necessary, but secondary. The primary reality is Christ in the assembly, the People of God."[15]

In his pastoral letter, *Dies Domini,* Pope John Paul II underlines the ecclesial dimension of the liturgical assembly as "the privileged place of unity,"[16] and stresses anew the conciliar agenda of full and active liturgical participation:

"There is a need, too, to ensure that all those present, children and adults, take an active interest, by encouraging their involvement at those points where the liturgy suggests and recommends it . . .

13. GIRM 62.

14. U.S. Bishops' Committee on the Liturgy, "Environment and Art in Catholic Worship" (Washington, D.C.: U.S. Catholic Conference, 1978) no. 28. See also The Pastoral Commentary on the Revised Sacramentary which states: "Christ is really present first of all in the assembly itself" (no. 5).

15. The Bishops' Committee on Priestly Life and Ministry, National Conference of Catholic Bishops, *Fulfilled in Your Hearing: The Homily in the Sunday Assembly* (Washington, D.C.: United States Catholic Conference, 1982) 4.

16. "Apostolic Letter *Dies Domini* of the Holy Father John Paul II to the Bishops, Clergy, and Faithful of the Catholic Church on Keeping the Lord's Day Holy" (31 May 1998) no. 36.

'offering the sacrifice and receiving holy communion, they take part actively in the liturgy,' finding in it light and strength to live their baptismal priesthood and the witness of a holy life."[17]

The Pope also notes the cultural challenges to maintaining Sunday as the day of the Lord, a day of celebration, and the obvious ways in which those challenges impede participation in the liturgical assembly.[18]

THE LITURGICAL ASSEMBLY
IN THE REVISED SACRAMENTARY
The Pastoral Introduction to the revised Sacramentary further emphasizes the liturgical assembly's singular act of worship and the diversity of roles in that body:

"Just as each organ and limb is necessary for the sound functioning of the body (see 1 Corinthians 12) so every member of the assembly has a part to play in the action of the whole." (no. 4)

Moreover, the Pastoral Introduction delineates three elements within the eucharistic celebration that foster unity in a significant way: (1) the dialogues between the assembly and ministers (including acclamations); (2) singing; and (3) uniformity in posture and gesture.[19]

Thus, as the assembly exercises its royal priesthood in the one sacrifice of praise (no. 6), it is once again the body of Christ convoked in holy assembly that celebrates and receives the Body of Christ: "the gifts of God for the people of God"[20]—at least in principle. But we must honestly admit that we are still finding our way as local churches struggle to discover what this means and what their liturgical participation demands of them when it is taken seriously. We are often left with more questions than answers. What is the proper balance between the universality of the tradition and the locality of the worshiping community? What is the relationship between the parish church and the local bishop; between the local church and the Bishop of Rome?

17. Ibid., no. 51.
18. Ibid., no. 4.
19. See John K. Leonard and Nathan D. Mitchell, *The Postures of the Assembly During the Eucharistic Prayer* (Chicago: Liturgy Training Publications, 1994).
20. See John D. Laurence, S.J., "The Assembly as Liturgical Symbol," *Louvain Studies* 22 (1997) 127–52. Laurence speaks of the liturgical assembly as the immediate human subject of the liturgy with Christ as the ultimate subject, in that it is Christ who ultimately acts through the gathered community (147–48).

As early as the fourth century, the tradition of the *fermentum*,[21] a small piece of the papal host from the principal stational Mass of the day that was placed in the chalice by the presbyters who led the Eucharist in the *tituli*, symbolized the unity between the local church and the Bishop of Rome. Today, despite the fact that the *fermentum* continues to be used in the liturgy, few people understand its significance. How can substantial unity within the Roman Rite be maintained while encouraging a liturgical pluralism where genuine cultural diversity is celebrated within a pluralistic Church?[22] These questions, of course, have ecclesial implications far beyond the realm of liturgical practice.

While the conciliar agenda has not changed, we find ourselves in a very different place today than at the time of the Second Vatican Council. Of course, it is the same body of Christ, the same "one, holy, catholic, and apostolic Church," but the faces have changed, and so have the issues and needs, the problems and tensions, that its constituents bring with them each time they gather together for worship. At the beginning of the twentieth century, 80 percent of all Christians were whites living in the Northern Hemisphere; by the year 2020, however, 80 percent of all Christians will be "people of color" living in the Southern Hemisphere. Clearly, our future is a global and multicultural Church where the vast majority of active members will be the working poor.[23]

If we have learned anything in these postconciliar years, we have come to understand the importance of hospitality within the liturgical assembly, making room for one another, especially for the newcomers among us. Indeed, as liturgical leader Robert Hovda noted some years ago: "Every specialized ministry participates in that common ministry of hospitality. But it is the church as a whole that is the host and basic minister of hospitality as of liturgy in general."[24]

21. See John F. Baldovin, S.J., *The Urban Character of Christian Worship: The Origins, Development, and Meaning of Stational Liturgy* (Rome: Orientalia Christiana Analecta, 1987) 121, 123.

22. See Anscar J. Chupungco, O.S.B., "Liturgical Pluralism in Multiethnic Communities," *Worship: Beyond Inculturation* (Washington, D.C.: The Pastoral Press, 1994) 160–61.

23. Nathan Mitchell, "What Is the Renewal That Awaits Us?" *The Renewal That Awaits Us,* ed. Eleanor Bernstein, C.S.J., and Martin F. Connell (Chicago: Liturgy Training Publications, 1996) 29.

24. Robert W. Hovda, "The Amen Corner: The Hospitality of the Liturgical Assembly," *Worship* 59 (1985) 438.

Liturgical hospitality will be crucially important as we consider the growing multicultural dimension of our communities. More than ever, the Church in the United States is an immigrant church. Consider the statistics. From 1990 to 1994, 4.5 million immigrants came to the United States, almost as many as arrived during the whole decade of the 1970s.[25] In 1995, the largest group of immigrants came from Mexico, followed by the former Soviet Union, the Philippines, Vietnam, the Dominican Republic, China, India, and Cuba.[26] These statistics are confirmed by a 1990 article in *Time* magazine, projecting that by the year 2056, "the 'average' U.S. resident, as defined by the census statistics, will trace his/her descent to Africa, Asia, the Hispanic world, the Pacific Islands, Arabia—almost anywhere but white Europe."[27]

While the immigrant groups are varied, the Hispanic presence is strong and continues to grow, especially in large urban areas. The nation's Hispanic population totaled 22.4 million in 1990, and an estimated 80 percent are Catholic. At the same time, pastoral leaders both in North and South America are concerned with a growing attraction among Hispanic Catholics toward Protestant fundamentalist and Pentecostal churches. An estimated 100,000 Hispanics per year are leaving the Church to join those churches, often in search of smaller, more intimate communities they are unable to find within large, urban, too often anonymous parishes.[28] Such issues are always complex and seldom lend themselves to quick solutions, but the lure toward Protestant fundamentalism does raise questions about the atmosphere created or not created in our liturgical assemblies and what we are or are not doing to create a hospitable environment for Hispanic Catholics.

Immigrant groups often bring with them a rich tradition of popular religiosity with special devotions, processions, and feasts that can too often be misunderstood by Anglo Catholics, especially when an

25. Steven A. Holmes, "A Surge in Immigration Surprises Experts and Intensifies a Debate," *The New York Times* (August 30, 1995) A1.

26. Lee Price, *Statistical Abstract of the United States 1997* (Washington, D.C.: U.S. Department of Commerce, Economics and Statistics Administration, Bureau of the Census, 1997).

27. Naushad Mehta and others, "Beyond the Melting Pot," *Time* 135 (15) (April 9, 1990) 38, as quoted in Mark R. Francis, C.S.V., "Who Is the Assembly Today?" *Assembly* 25 (2) (March 1999) 2ff.

28. Felician A. Foy, O.F.M., and Rose M. Avato, *Catholic Almanac 1998* (Huntington, Ind.: Our Sunday Visitor, 1997) 492.

attempt is made to include expressions of popular religion within the liturgy itself. Immediately after the council, liturgists were quick to dismiss such manifestations of popular devotion as inappropriate or superstitious, or as impeding "full and active liturgical participation," much to the consternation of catechists and other pastoral agents. Today, there is a renewed desire to better understand the role that popular religion plays in the lives of these different cultural groups, toward a more informed study of the relationship between liturgy and popular religiosity.[29]

Increasing numbers of parishes, especially in big cities like Chicago, Los Angeles, Miami, New York, Toronto, and Vancouver, find themselves in multicultural situations where a number of different cultural groups share membership in the same local parish. While this offers tremendous opportunities for a rich cultural exchange and a beautiful manifestation of the diversity of cultures and gifts within the one body of Christ, it also presents challenges. In a recent pastoral letter on the liturgy, Cardinal Roger Mahony of Los Angeles notes:

"Yes, we want liturgy with sounds and gestures that flow from the religious soul of a people, whether Vietnamese or Mexican, Native American or African American. Yet we have a Catholic soul. We are in need of witnessing to that soul, of being in assemblies where the vision of Paul comes alive, where the Vietnamese, the Mexican, the Native American and African American stand side by side around the table singing one thanksgiving to God. And although that thanksgiving may have the rhythm of one particular culture, all will join with their hearts. Before we are anything else—any sex, ethnicity, nationality or citizenship—we need to be the Body of Christ, sisters and brothers by our Baptism. Every one of us needs to know by heart some of the music, vocabulary, movement, and ways of thinking and feeling that are not of our own background. The larger society we are a part of needs this witness."[30]

When Martin Hellriegel challenged the melting pot theory earlier in this century, he was ahead of his time. Hellriegel's vision of liturgical assemblies as a cultural mosaic is truer today than it has ever

29. See Anscar J. Chupungco, *Liturgical Inculturation: Sacramentals, Religiosity, and Catechesis* (Collegeville: The Liturgical Press, 1992).

30. Cardinal Roger Mahony, "Gather Faithfully Together: Guide for Sunday Mass" (Chicago: Liturgy Training Publications, 1997) no. 29.

been. But maintaining the balance between diversity in all its forms while upholding the fundamental unity of the Roman Rite presents all sorts of challenges for liturgists and pastoral leaders. Cardinal Mahony continues:

"This striving for catholicity extends beyond ethnicity: the Sunday assembly should bring together men, women and children of all ages. It should be the one experience in our lives when we will not be sorted out by education level, skin color, intelligence, politics, sexual orientation, wealth or lack of it, or any other human condition. If the assembly is the basic symbol when the liturgy is celebrated (Catechism of the Catholic Church, 1188), the comfortable homogeneity promoted by so many in this nation has no place. Homogeneity and comfort are not Gospel values."[31]

While it is true that assemblies should not be sorted out by categories and social groupings, it is also true that the particular needs and issues within that cultural mosaic of the liturgical assembly should not be ignored. Within Euro-American Catholic communities, for example, the assembly is increasingly better educated with growing numbers of Catholics holding undergraduate and graduate degrees, unlike the early years of this century. Many of these men and women are increasingly trained in theology as well. They have come to expect a level of competence among liturgical ministers that is commensurate with what they find in medicine, law, or banking. Taking the Sunday homily as an example, they expect preaching that is well prepared and articulate, capable of addressing the problems in their own lives, and they can easily identify preaching that is unprepared, superficial, or patronizing.

There are increasing numbers of ecumenical and interreligious marriages. Of course, ecumenical and interreligious families have always existed, but their presence today is more common and calls for greater pastoral sensitivity and hospitality within the Sunday assembly.

As a microcosm of secular society, all the realities and challenges facing life in North America will be present, to a greater or lesser degree, within the Church itself. For example, the number of divorces in the United States has grown from 479,000 in 1965 to 1,169,000 in 1994.[32] Statisticians inform us that as many as 50 percent of all

31. Ibid., no. 33.
32. Price, *Statistical Abstract of the United States.*

marriages performed today will end in divorce. We can lament this sad reality, but at the same time we must find ways of reaching out pastorally to increasing numbers of Catholic families touched by divorce and to divorced and remarried Catholics themselves, so that they are not made to feel like pariahs in our liturgical assemblies. Add to the list the growing number of single-parent families; gay and lesbian Catholics; those who struggle with addictions and disease; the unemployed and the homeless.

The impact of the media upon American culture offers one of the greatest challenges to the liturgical assembly. In a new world of cyberspace that changes by the minute with shopping on the Internet along with everything else one could imagine, in a world of video games and rock videos, ATM machines and fast food, ours is an age that craves entertainment and instant gratification. While liturgy should engage its participants, it is not about entertainment or "what I get out of it." Yet our media-conscious culture does its best to seduce even the most devout believers.

Cardinal Mahony remarks:

"In the past generation, we have introduced into the liturgy some practices and attitudes from North American society that have no place there. For example: the hurried pace, the tyranny of the clock, the inattention to the arts, the casual tone of a presider, the 'what can I get out of it?' approach of the consumer, the 'entertain me' attitude of a nation of television watchers. All these are the wrong sort of inculturation. Their prevalence shows how difficult it is to seek what in the culture offers a true correspondence with the spirit of the Liturgy."[33]

The Second Vatican Council called the Church to listen to the signs of the times. While the fundamental vision of "full and active participation" remains as much a goal today as it was thirty-five years ago, that goal will need to be reinterpreted again and again as the face of the Mystical Body of Christ continues to change and new patterns of ritual behavior emerge. New models will need to be employed if we are to respond effectively to changing pastoral needs, such as the growing number of Sunday assemblies in Canada and the United States without a resident priest.[34] In *Dies Domini*, Pope John Paul II

33. Mahony, "Gather Faithfully Together," no. 34.
34. See James Dallen, *The Dilemma of Priestless Sundays* (Chicago: Liturgy Training Publications, 1994); Kathleen Hughes, R.S.C.J., "Sunday Celebrations

writes: "In situations where the Eucharist cannot be celebrated, the Church recommends that the Sunday assembly come together even without a priest. . . ."[35] Just what those assemblies do when they come together is less clear-cut, despite the help given by the Congregation for Divine Worship's 1988 *Directory for Sunday Celebrations in the Absence of a Priest* and the 1993 ritual book for such occasions published by the bishops of the United States.

CONCLUSION

Almost forty years after the council, we now have a participative liturgy in most places, but the quality and the results of those liturgies differ drastically, as does the self-identity and commitment of the liturgical assembly. The challenge remains to discover the full meaning of the assembly's central role in the liturgy and the relationship of liturgical participation to care for the poor and needy. Even despite our best efforts, the individualism and narcissism within our culture can too easily find its way into our liturgical assemblies as well. Thus, people can participate liturgically week after week, and yet leave the doors of that assembly apparently unchanged, not longing for the reign of God any more today than yesterday, or last month, or last year. As Jesuit liturgist John Laurence rightly notes: "liturgical assemblies are authentic signs of Christ's universal love only to the degree that as symbols they embody, and are committed to embody beyond the liturgy, reverence for all God's children and full justice in the world."[36]

Assemblies need to look beyond themselves, beyond the confines of their own church buildings, but that care for the needy and those on the fringe must begin within the assembly itself. We cannot expect great success at caring for the needs of the poor and homeless in the streets if we are unable first to address the needs of those to our left and right, front and back, in the assembly itself. Communities that are divided outside the Sunday assembly over all sorts of issues will not find those tensions miraculously vanishing upon entrance into the church vestibule on Sunday morning. Washed in the waters of baptism, we became brothers and sisters of Christ and of one another.

---

in the Absence of a Priest: Some Disquieting Reflections," *New Theology Review* 8 (1) (February 1995) 45–57.

35. *Dies Domini*, no. 53.

36. Laurence, "The Assembly as Liturgical Symbol," 147.

Nourished at the holy table, we are strengthened to live out that call to be sister and brother to one another.

Calling the Sunday Eucharist "the primary manifestation of the local Church," the Pastoral Introduction to the Revised Sacramentary notes: "It should be in every sense inclusive [and not needlessly multiplied]" (no. 4). The Pastoral Introduction continues: "The very arrangement of the celebration in its various ministries shows that all the baptized have a place in the Church: women and men, the young and old, people of every race and way of life" (no. 8). Thus, the importance of hospitality and reverence for one another within the assembly cannot be underestimated, especially for the weaker members: the sick and elderly; the handicapped; parents with infants.

Several years ago, the superior of a community of retired and infirm priests was presiding at the Mass of the Lord's Supper on Holy Thursday evening. During the first reading, he noticed the door of the crowded chapel open, and an old priest was brought in and left in the back, seated in his wheelchair. Immediately, the presider got up from his chair, walked to the back of the chapel, and wheeled the man to the front so that he would have a full view of everything taking place. Afterwards, someone remarked: "There was no need for the homily or the washing of the feet. That one gesture on the part of the presider spoke volumes." Such hospitality, of course, is not the responsibility of the presider alone, but should mark the whole assembly.

In a recent article on the liturgical assembly, my colleague Mark Francis frames some important questions:

"Does the environment for worship and the liturgical ministers serving the assembly reflect the rich diversity of the parish? Is it possible for someone in a wheel chair to proclaim a Scripture reading? Does the iconography and devotional spaces of the church present people of holiness reflective of the cultures and races of the community? Is the music sensitive to the varied musical styles of the cultures which compose the assembly? Do the examples and illustrations used in the homily go beyond the confines of one particular group and consciously encompass the wider range of experiences of the women and men of the parish? How are young people involved in an active and appropriate way in the liturgical action?"[37]

37. Francis, "Who Is the Assembly Today?" 5.

Like the first-century disciples of Jesus or Augustine's fourth-century community in North Africa, the Mystical Body of Christ remains a motley bunch, and so, too, the liturgical assembly—a community of "graced sinners," always incomplete as we "wait in joyful hope." The rough edges and the tensions remain as they did at the very beginning; even the Internet can't change that.

United together around word and sacrament, there is no room for distinctions between the haves and the have-nots, between different cultural groups; no room for competition among ministers or for "performances" that call more attention to the minister than to the liturgical act itself; no room for division in the assembly among those who squabble over such things that pale in comparison to the reign of God for which we long. Rather, the liturgical assembly must be a "communion of complementary charisms,"[38] instruments of transformation for the churches, and indeed, for the whole human family.

38. Laurence, "The Assembly as Liturgical Symbols," 141.

Mark R. Francis, C.S.V.

Well Begun Is Half Done: The New Introductory Rites in the Revised Sacramentary

The beginning of the present Order of Mass has been the object of much scholarly and pastoral discussion since the *editio typica* of the Missal of Paul VI was promulgated in 1969.[1] As a ritual unit, the introductory rites have been criticized as unnecessarily complicated and unwieldy. Both scholarly and pastoral critique of these rites led ICEL to focus on the beginning of Mass in the 1986 consultation with the English-speaking conferences of bishops. A series of ritual options practically identical to those provided in the revised Sacramentary were contained in ICEL's second progress report (September 1990). Subsequent to that consultation, ICEL received formal requests from several bishops' conferences to include these alternatives in the revision of the Sacramentary in order to make the introductory rites more pastorally effective.

1. Robert Cabié, "Le nouvel ordo missae," *La Maison-Dieu* 100 (1969) 21–35; Emil J. Lengeling, *Die neue Ordnung der Eucharistiefeier. Kommentar der Dokumente zum Römischen Messbuch* (Leipzig, 1970) 198–99; Ralph Keifer, "Our Cluttered Vestibule: The Unreformed Entrance Rite," *Worship* 48 (1974) 270–77; Kenneth Smits, "A Congregational Order of Worship," *Worship* 54 (1980) 55–75; Gabe Huck, "Introductory Rites at the Lord's Supper: The First, Best Moments," *Liturgy* 1 (4) (1981) 13–19; Charles Gusmer, "Reviewing the Order of Mass," *Worship* 57 (1983) 345–48; John Baldovin, "Kyrie Eleison and the Entrance Rite," *Worship* 60 (1986) 334–47; Mark Searle, "The Opening and Closing Rites of the Mass," *Shaping English Liturgy: Studies in Honor of Archbishop Denis Hurley,* ed. Peter Finn and James Schellman (Washington, D.C.: The Pastoral Press, 1990) 53–92; Michael G. Witczak, "The Introductory Rites: Threshold of the Sacred, Entry into Community, or Pastoral Problem?" *Liturgical Ministry* 3 (1994) 22–27; Mark Francis, "Uncluttering the Eucharistic Vestibule: The Entrance Rites through Time," *Liturgical Ministry* 3 (1994) 1–12.

The six new alternatives are based on the *Missale Romanum* and on the approved edition of the Sacramentary used by other language groups, especially the German *Messbuch* (1975). These variations are informed by the growing literature on the history and theology of the introductory rites at Mass. In his proposal for a ferial Order of Mass, Anscar Chupungco has contributed to this study by proposing a more intentional application of the concept of "progressive solemnity."[2] This principle as described in the liturgical documents "takes into account the abilities of the assembly, the relative importance of the individual rites and their constituent parts, and the relative festivity of the liturgical day."[3] As he points out in this study, Vatican II has inspired an entirely different understanding of "festivity" or liturgical solemnity than the juridical and rubrical notion that held sway in the Missal of Pius V. The liturgical reform of Vatican II, expressed in the Constitution on the Sacred Liturgy, promotes a much more theological basis for solemnity linked to the nature of the worshiping assembly and the liturgical year. ICEL's six alternatives for the opening rites are faithful to the historical variation of the rites as well as to this notion of progressive solemnity announced in the liturgical documents and further elucidated by scholars such as Chupungco.

The modest aim of this present commentary is to look specifically at the new introductory rites through much the same lens. The six new variations of the introductory rites in the revised Sacramentary will be discussed in light of their nature and function announced by the GIRM and the Introduction to the Order of Mass prepared by ICEL for the revised Sacramentary.

THE ELEMENTS AND PURPOSE OF THE INTRODUCTORY RITES AT MASS

In order to appreciate the rearrangement and development of the opening rites of the Mass as presented in the revision, it is helpful to first identify their various elements as presented in the 1969 Sacramentary. The General Instruction on the Roman Missal (GIRM 24) names the introductory rites as "the entrance song, greeting, penitential rite, *Kyrie, Gloria,* and opening prayer or collect." This listing,

2. "Toward a Ferial Order of Mass," *Ecclesia Orans* 10 (1) (1993) 11–32.
3. *Liturgical Music Today,* 13, *The Liturgy Documents: A Parish Resource,* 3rd ed. (Chicago: Liturgy Training Publications, 1991) 299.

however, needs further elaboration in order to appreciate the complexity of the ritual elements presented in the 1969 Sacramentary. What is not specifically mentioned is the entrance procession of the ministers while the entrance song is sung, the veneration of the altar by the priest and deacon, and the Sign of the Cross led by the priest— all of which precede the initial greeting and response of the assembly. Following the greeting, the rite also encourages the presider to offer a monition introducing the Mass of the day (GIRM 29). Furthermore, in place of the penitential rite and *Kyrie,* a rite of blessing and sprinkling of water may be used. Both the sprinkling or the penitential rite precede the *Gloria* on Sundays and feasts outside of Advent and Lent. Finally, one must consider the invitation to pray voiced by the presider, followed by a silence which introduced the collect or opening prayer. These ritual elements, not specifically named in GIRM 24, need also to be taken into account when studying the revision of the present introductory rites.

Having identified the elements, what is the purpose of the introductory rites? The GIRM stipulates that they have "the character of beginning, introduction and preparation" for what is to follow and goes on to declare that "the purpose of these rites is to make the assembled people a unified community and to prepare them properly to listen to God's word and celebrate the eucharist" (24). The new Introduction to the Order of Mass provided in the revised Missal which is meant to supplement what is already contained in the GIRM (7, 24) more fully explains the purpose of the introductory rites by grounding them firmly in the theology of the liturgical assembly as the epiphany of Christ's presence.

"In the introductory rites the assembly is called together in Christ and established again as Church. The Risen Lord is present in the midst of the assembly, which becomes visible as the body of Christ. Thus, the assembly itself is the first instance of Christ's presence in the liturgy. The function of these rites is to enable the community coming together from a multiplicity of concerns and variety of ways of life, to become aware of itself again as a gathered community, alert and ready to listen to the word and celebrate the sacrament" (66).

One of the principal criteria, then, for judging the effectiveness of the introductory rites is how well or how poorly they help the assembly become conscious of its identity as Christ's body and prepare for the hearing of the Word. It is reasonable to assume, then, that the choice of one of the six variants proposed in the revised Sacramentary is to be based on both the needs of the assembly and the liturgical season. Before moving to a review of these six alternative introductory rites, a comment on the rites leading up to and including the greeting and opening dialogue is called for.

THE ENTRANCE RITES

Both the GIRM and the new Introduction to the Sacramentary assume that the assembly's worship will begin with a song and procession of ministers to the sanctuary. We know that this mode of beginning the eucharistic celebration dates from the "classical" period of the Roman Rite of the sixth and seventh centuries. Influenced by the papal liturgy of the Eternal City (which in turn borrowed heavily from imperial court ceremonial) the presider, with the entourage of ministers, enters into the basilica and moves through the assembly in solemn procession accompanied by the schola's chant of the introit psalm.[4] As some have pointed out, this was the beginning of a clericalization of the rite that would continue during the Middle Ages and Tridentine period and placed the focus of the rite almost entirely on the priest to the exclusion of the rest of the assembly. This clericalization reached its apogee after the Council of Trent, when the procession through the assembly was effectively eliminated, since in many countries "low Mass" was the normative celebration. The common way Mass began prior to the council was the entrance of the priest with one or two servers from the side door of a sacristy located next to the sanctuary.

The "classical," "imperial" entrance was re-proposed by the 1969 Missal as the normative way of beginning the celebration. The priest and ministers' procession from the back of the church while the opening song is sung by those present emphasizes the assembly's participation in the beginning of the liturgy in a way that it had not been since the sixth century. The new Introduction affirms that the opening song and procession is meant to help the assembly "create an ambience of celebration, a sense of identity, and an awareness of the mystery being unfolded" (67).

All this being said, it is obvious that the way in which we begin the celebration is still rather centered on the priest. How we name this part of the Eucharist is important. The "entrance" procession and the

4. See Theodor Klauser, *A Short History of the Western Liturgy*, trans. John Halliburton (Oxford: Oxford University Press, 1979) 59–62, and Mark R. Francis, "Uncluttering the Eucharistic Vestibule," 6–8.

"entrance" song is called such because it is the priest and the ministers who are entering. Although actively involved by singing the opening song, the assembly—which is supposed to be the subject and primary agent of the liturgical action—is essentially witnessing the entrance of the priest. In those parishes still employing commentators, it is not unusual to hear their invitation to the assembly to sing the opening hymn with the ritual directive, "Let us now rise to greet Father by singing . . ." While clearly this is not the official intent of the rite, these commentators ought to be forgiven their statement of the "ritual reality."

The new Introduction seeks to attenuate this interpretation by stressing that the procession of ministers is "through and from the assembly" (67). One can infer from this phrase that there is an encouragement here to include other members of the assembly in addition to the priest and other liturgical ministers in the entrance procession. However this "imperial" form of entrance when wedded to an "entertainment" style of presiding can lead to an unwitting clericalization of the liturgy.[5] After a focus on the priest's entrance, if the celebration is begun by introductory comments of the presider such as "Good morning . . . and isn't this a beautiful morning!" or "I'm surprised any one made it to church today, it's so cold!" the sense of transcendence and the ritual relationship between presider and assembly is obscured. If care is not taken to help the assembly feel a part of the liturgical action at this point of the celebration, the "entrance procession" can create a worship experience that is more clerical than the Tridentine Rite it was meant to correct. Many commentators speak in a more inclusive way of "gathering rites" and "gathering" songs during this part of the Mass as if we are referring to the whole assembly as coming together. However, given the way the present rite is usually enacted, it is still really more accurate to say that we are witnessing and participating in the entrance of the priest and the other ministers.

SIGN OF THE CROSS, GREETING, AND INTRODUCTION

After the veneration of the altar, the priest goes to the chair and makes the Sign of the Cross with the people. Paul VI insisted on retaining the Sign of the Cross as the way to begin Mass.[6] It should be recalled that this manner of starting Mass dates only from the Middle Ages when

5. See, for example, Robert Hurd, "A More Organic Opening: Ritual Music and the New Gathering Rite," *Worship* 72 (1998) 294.
6. Francis, "Uncluttering the Eucharistic Vestibule," 10, 11.

the priest and servers prepared themselves for the eucharistic celebration by saying the "Prayers at the Foot of the Altar" which, as private prayer, began with the Sign of the Cross. For this reason there
exists a kind of trinitarian "doublet" in the present rite: we invoke
the Trinity with the Sign of the Cross and then are often greeted by
the presider with one of a number of possible trinitarian invocations
such as "The grace of our Lord Jesus Christ, the Love of God, and the
fellowship of the Holy Spirit be with you all." This redundancy is unfortunate. I have speculated elsewhere that this rather abrupt verbal
beginning leads to an understandable yet mistaken desire on the part
of presiders to "introduce" the introductory Sign of the Cross such as
"let us begin this Mass as we begin all prayer, 'In the name of the
Father . . .'" This statement is patently not true if, as the new Introduction asserts, "the assembly's worship begins with the opening
song and procession" (67). Clearly, if Mass were begun with a greeting, there would be less of a tendency for presiders to add unneces-
sary verbiage to provide a kind of greeting before the Sign of the
Cross and the following liturgical greeting.

The presider (or "occasionally the deacon or another member of
the assembly") then introduces the Mass of the day (Introduction 70).
The new Introduction points out the crucial importance of this monition by noting that "a very brief and well-prepared comment can
help to create the appropriate atmosphere and give tone and orientation to the entire celebration" (70). There is also the helpful suggestion that "strangers, guests and special groups" be welcomed at this
point and, if there are a significant number of children, that they be
directly addressed during these comments. These pastoral directives
underline the importance of acknowledging those who are gathered
as the body of Christ. Since this acknowledgment constitutes a concrete gesture of welcome and hospitality it will also depend largely
on the cultural background of those who have gathered. Involving
the whole assembly in a greeting and welcome of those present may
also be appropriate at this point in the celebration.

NEW OPENING RITES—SIX POSSIBILITIES
The six alternatives for the opening rites provided in the revised
Sacramentary can be schematized as follows:

I. Rite of Blessing and Sprinkling of Water
   (without absolution prayer)

II. Penitential Rite

(Form A or B of the present Penitential Rite with absolution prayer but no Kyrie)

III. Litany of Praise

(Form C of the present Penitential Rite which focuses on praising Christ rather than repentance; no absolution prayer)

IV. Kyrie

V. Gloria

(May be used in addition to another opening rite; not to be used during Advent and Lent)

VI. Other Opening Rites

(For example, when the Eucharist is combined with Liturgy of the Hours, Baptism, Marriage; on Passion Sunday)

All of these alternatives serve to give a single ritual focus where before there were several sometimes conflicting elements. This revision is meant to help the assembly take a more active part in the introductory rites and provide a more streamlined way of preparing to hear the readings. A glance at each of the options reveals this underlying pastoral intent of these alternatives.

RITE OF BLESSING AND SPRINKLING OF WATER

As in the 1970 English version of the Sacramentary, the rite of blessing and sprinkling of water is the first opening rite presented. Its placement in the Sacramentary is significant. Unlike some of the other modern-language Sacramentaries (the French or the *texto unificado* version of the Spanish Sacramentary) that relegate this option to an appendix at the back of the book, the blessing and sprinkling of water appears as an important option in the 1970 edition and again in the revised ICEL Sacramentary. Because of its emphasis on Easter and baptism, it again is highlighted as an appropriate way to begin the Mass during the Easter season (Introduction 72)

At first glance this alternative appears much the same as it does in the previous versions of the Sacramentary, but there is an important addition to the present rite. First, a new chanted version of the blessing is provided (version C) which involves the people at the beginning of the blessing in a litany with the presider.

"Praise be the Lord the Creator.
   R. Praised be the name of the Lord.

Praised be the Lord, the Resurrection and the life.
   R. Praised be the name of the Lord.

Praised be the Lord, the Spirit of holiness.
   R. Praised be the name of the Lord."

The rest of the texts are essentially the same except that there is no longer an absolution prayer which ends the rites once the ministers and the people have been sprinkled. Rather, the opening prayer or collect serves as the conclusion to the sprinkling rite; the absolution prayer has been eliminated. This, too, is a significant development. As Bob Hurd has pointed out, the 1970 sprinkling rite "is more like a *variation* on the penitential rite than a real *alternative* to it. The wording of the prayers emphasizes the washing away of sins and the sprinkling ends—as does the penitential rite—with an absolution text."[7] Now the focus is principally on the blessing and sprinkling as "a memorial of Easter and baptism. God is thanked for intervening to save us through the medium of water and is asked to continue to give forgiveness and life" (Introduction 72). Ritually, it is also more straightforward. Instead of having two presidential prayers back to back (the old absolution prayer before the opening prayer), the first has been wisely omitted in order to allow the assembly to focus on what is the much more important of the two texts.

Finally, the revised Sacramentary also allows for a further important variation. If the greeting and blessing of the water are to take place at the door of the church, the sprinkling of the people is to take place during the entrance procession (Introduction 72). The advantage to this ritual option would seem to be that it would both streamline the introductory rite, allowing the assembly a paced and prayerful contemplation of the resurrection of Christ and their baptismal dignity, and attenuate the sometimes unfortunate emphasis on the presider's entrance which we have spoken of earlier.

PENITENTIAL RITE

There are two variations for the penitential rite in the revised Sacramentary: Form A (the old *Confiteor*) and Form B (the dialogue based on Psalms 50 [51] and 85). As we noted above, the *Confiteor* as part of

7. Hurd, "A More Organic Opening," 300.

the series of medieval prayers said at "the foot of the altar" in the Tridentine Rite was not technically part of the Mass but served as the personal preparation of the priest and servers before going to the altar. This prayer only became an official part of the Mass Rite at the insistence of Paul VI in 1969. As scholars have pointed out, its emphasis on confession of sins and intercession to God through the prayers of Mary, the saints, and the congregation is not necessarily the most theologically significant or logical way of preparing to "celebrate the sacred mysteries."[8] Be that as it may, this time-honored prayer, at least when said by all present, includes the assembly in an act of repentance. Crucial to its effectiveness, of course, is that time be given for silent reflection after the initial invitation to "call to mind our sins."

The second variation has been amended to do away with the confusion that often resulted from the 1970 invocation, "Lord we have sinned against you. Lord, have mercy. R. Lord, have mercy." This form often led the assembly to believe that the presider was beginning the old form C (The "Lord, have mercy" with tropes). As a result, many presiders avoided this version of the penitential rite altogether. The present arrangement begins rather with "Have mercy, Lord," with the people's response, "For we have sinned against you," thus obviating the confusion. It should also be noted that another minister may now offer this penitential dialogue with the assembly. This practice parallels the possibility of another minister voicing the invocations in the old form C.

Both variations on the penitential rite are followed by one of two absolution prayers by the priest. The first is the familiar: May almighty God have mercy on us, forgive us our sins, and bring us to life everlasting. The second possible absolution formula is the absolution that was formerly given at the end of the sprinkling rite, and now repositioned as an alternative here. The Introduction in the revised Sacramentary logically recommends either form of the penitential rite for the season of Lent (Introduction 73).

LITANY OF PRAISE, *KYRIE*

Of all the current "penitential rites" form C in the present Sacramentary employing the expression "Lord, have mercy" has been most

8. See, for example, Ralph Keifer, *To Give Thanks and Praise: General Instruction of the Roman Missal* (Washington, D.C.: Pastoral Press, 1980) 111–15.

often misunderstood. The litanic response "Lord, have mercy" has often been interpreted by presiders as exclusively penitential, beseeching God for forgiveness for the sins we have committed. Due to this misinterpretation, and despite the sample tropes or invocations provided in the current Sacramentary, this moment in the rite has often been used by presiders as a kind of examination of conscience—"For the times we have been unfaithful to the demands of the Gospel . . . Lord, have mercy."

The meaning of "Lord, have mercy" becomes clearer when we consider that it originated in the Greek-speaking church as a response to a litany that took place at the beginning of the Divine (Eucharistic) Liturgy at which the mercy of God was invoked upon the assembly, the larger Church, and the world. In its origins it had nothing to do with the penitential *Confiteor*, but was a separate element of the rite. This fact helps us to make sense of the fact that its emphasis is not on us (our sinfulness) but on God's mercy and salvific action in Jesus Christ. It could be just as accurately translated "O Lord, you are merciful!" Note that the sample tropes all center on what Christ has done for us, not how we have sinned. For example, "you were sent to heal the contrite," "you have shown us the way to the Father," or "you come in word and sacrament to strengthen us in holiness." As the Introduction notes: "The litany of praise is addressed to Christ our Redeemer. A number of models are offered for imitation and adaptation. All such adaptation should, like the models provided, focus on Christ and his mercy."

For this reason this alternative is now more accurately entitled "Litany of Praise" and no longer ends with the absolution text but concludes with the opening prayer. The invitation also makes the doxological nature of this introductory rite clearer. For example: "Before listening to the word and celebrating the eucharist, let us praise the Lord Jesus Christ."

The emphasis of the following alternative, the *Kyrie* or "Lord, have mercy" without the tropes, is also on praise of Christ, not penance. Its sample introductions all end with the imperative "Acclaim Christ our Savior." As a traditional chant of the Roman Rite, the *Kyrie eleison*, or "Lord, have mercy" as a fourth alternative introductory rite is clearly meant to be sung by the assembly, alternating with the cantor and the choir (Introduction 75). Like the "Lord, have mercy" with tropes, it no longer concludes with the absolution prayer, but with the opening prayer.

GLORIA

The fifth alternative opening rite is the freestanding use of the *Gloria* as an exceptionally festive way of beginning the eucharistic celebration. This ancient hymn was originally imported from the Byzantine *Orthros* or morning prayer on Sunday to solemnize the Pope's Mass at Christmas since it begins with the angels' joyous acclamation of praise at the birth of Christ from Luke 2:14, "Glory to God in the highest and peace to God's people on earth." Its use later became extended until it became a fixed text for all Sunday and festive Masses outside of Lent and Advent. The revised Sacramentary returns to its original application in the Roman Rite by proposing its use as a way of emphasizing the high seasons of the Church year such as Eastertide and Christmastide. These times naturally call for a solemn and festive way of beginning the celebration that focuses on our praise of God for the incarnation and resurrection of Jesus. Logically, the discipline continues that this option is not to be used during the penitential seasons of Advent and Lent. As a hymn, the clear preference is that it always be sung "entirely, or in part, by the people" (Introduction 76).

OTHER OPENING RITES

The last alternative provided by the revised Sacramentary simply notes that "another opening rite may be selected for particular occasions and in accord with the prescriptions of the respective liturgical books" (Introduction 77). This provision is really no change from the present discipline since the introductory rites are modified at the celebration of ritual Masses such as baptism, marriage, and funerals to correspond to the rite being celebrated. Also, whenever there is a more elaborate entrance procession prescribed to begin Mass for feasts such as the Presentation of the Lord (Candlemas) and Passion or Palm Sunday the usual introductory rites are already abbreviated. Also, when the Liturgy of the Hours is celebrated with the Eucharist, the introductory rites are also modified to accommodate that celebration.

CONCLUSION

Each of the introductory-rite options presented in the revised Sacramentary serve to simplify what has often been a ritually complex and often unfocused moment of the celebration. Using the 1970 edition of the Sacramentary, it was not at all uncommon to experience (at least from the texts) a wild emotional swing from abject contrition to overflowing praise in a matter of seconds. By simplifying the options and more clearly emphasizing a particular approach for constituting the liturgical assembly as Christ's body and readying those gathered to hear God's word, the pastoral value of these various options is obvious. Moreover, linking the options more intentionally to the Liturgical Year has also helped to rescue the introductory rites from what has often been experienced as a set of rites that floats free and unattached to what follows.

Margaret Mary Kelleher, O.S.U.

New Prayer Texts in the Revised Sacramentary

In 1979 Karl Rahner offered a fundamental theological interpretation of the Second Vatican Council in which he proposed that it was "in a rudimentary form still groping for identity, the Church's first official self-actualization *as* a world Church."[1] In elaborating his thesis he held out the "victory of the vernacular in the Church's liturgy" as an unmistakable signal of "the coming-to-be of a world Church."[2] He was aware that the liturgical pluralism consonant with the emergence of a world church would be much more comprehensive than a move to the vernacular, and he knew that a process of inculturation involving many aspects of ecclesial life would be essential. Anscar Chupungco, who is being honored in this collection of essays, has made a major contribution in the area of liturgical inculturation through his research and writing, his teaching, his creative work in the Philippines, and as a member of the International Commission on English in the Liturgy. He has offered a direction for the ongoing process in which a world Church will be realized through the liturgy.

While Rahner's immediate concern was with the Church's passage from being a Western Church to becoming a world Church, his vision of such a Church was one of reciprocity. A world Church, in his mind, was one "which begins to act through the reciprocal influence exercised by all its components."[3] He knew that the realization of such a Church would have implications for theology, canon law, and ecclesiastical structures, but I find the attention he gave to the vernacular to be quite significant. In the thirty-five years since the promulgation of

1. Karl Rahner, S.J., "Towards a Fundamental Theological Interpretation of Vatican II," *Theological Studies* 40 (1979) 717.
2. Ibid., 719.
3. Ibid., 717.

Sacrosanctum concilium and the opening it gave to the use of the vernacular in liturgical prayer, churches throughout the world have been exploring what it means to pray in their native languages. They have realized that a move to the vernacular is a move into cultural worlds very different from the world of Latin compositions. Since the Second Vatican Council gave special recognition to the liturgy as an event in which the Church is disclosed, the composition of new prayer texts for the revised Sacramentary can be regarded as another step in the dynamic process by which a world Church is being actualized.[4]

BACKGROUND

The story of any church learning to pray in the vernacular is a piece of the story of the self-realization of a world Church. The English-speaking churches throughout the world began collaborating on this task during Vatican II and have been doing so ever since then through the work of the International Commission on English in the Liturgy.[5] A formal mandate was adopted in 1964 by the sponsoring conferences of bishops and addressed to the International Advisory Committee which was established to plan and supervise the work. It is interesting to note that the mandate directed the Advisory Committee "to work out a plan for the translation of liturgical texts and the provision of original texts where required in language which would be correct, dignified, intelligible, and suitable for public recitation and singing."[6] This visionary recognition of the need for original texts would be affirmed five years later in an instruction issued by the Apostolic See which stated that "texts translated from another language are clearly not sufficient for the celebration of a fully renewed liturgy. The creation of new texts will be necessary."[7]

ICEL's first step toward composing prayers in English is evident in the alternative opening prayers of the 1973 English version of the

4. See, for example, *Sacrosanctum concilium* 2 and 26. English translation by the International Commission on English in the Liturgy, in *Documents on the Liturgy: 1963–1979 Conciliar, Papal and Curial Texts* [hereafter DOL] (Collegeville: The Liturgical Press, 1982).

5. See Frederick R. McManus, "ICEL: The First Years," *Shaping English Liturgy: Studies in Honor of Archbishop Denis Hurley*, ed. Peter C. Finn and James M. Schellman (Washington, D.C.: Pastoral Press, 1990) 433–59.

6. Ibid., 447.

7. Consilium for the Implementation of the Constitution on the Liturgy, Instruction on the Translation of Liturgical Texts *Comme le prévoit*, 25 January 1969, no. 43: *Notitiae* 5 (1969) 3–12. English translation in DOL 123:880.

Sacramentary.[8] Inspiration came from the 1969 instruction which continued the statement quoted above regarding the need for new texts by saying that "translation of texts transmitted through the tradition of the Church is the best school and discipline for the creation of new texts so 'that any new forms adopted should in some way grow organically from forms already in existence' (SC art. 23)."[9] The initial experience of trying to translate the Latin prayer texts into English was a difficult and frustrating one and suggested the desirability of having an alternative style of prayer. A sample collection of alternative opening prayers was sent to all the bishops whose conferences were participants in ICEL. While the Latin text was used as the point of departure for these prayers, the texts elaborated upon the Latin in various ways. They were inspired by the Latin but not confined to its style.

The results of this consultation led the Episcopal Board of ICEL to authorize the composition of alternative opening prayers. As the project proceeded, a collection of fifteen alternative prayers was reviewed by ICEL's Advisory Committee and a number of consultants who offered a rigorous critique. The issues that arose in the consultation give an indication of the difficulties encountered in trying to find an appropriate style for prayer. While there was clearly a desire to incorporate new imagery in English prayers there were questions about just how much diversity could be sustained in one prayer. Prayers were criticized for their lack of logic, for being too sentimental, for being too long, for having too many adjectives. A second draft was produced along with a new series of prayers and the consultation process was again put in place. This led to a third draft which would later be subjected to further review and revisions. Eventually, a set of alternative opening prayers for Sundays and certain feasts was approved by the Advisory Committee, the Episcopal Board, and the various conferences of bishops. In the process of obtaining Roman confirmation the Congregation for the Doctrine of the Faith made suggestions for changing seven of the alternative prayers. After ICEL made some editorial changes in these texts, the Congregation for Divine Worship gave the confirmation to the Sacramentary which

8. For a detailed account of ICEL's work on original compositions from its beginnings through the early stages of the revised Sacramentary see H. Kathleen Hughes, R.S.C.J., "Original Texts: Beginnings, Present Projects, Guidelines," *Shaping English Liturgy*, 219–55. I rely on her work for what follows on alternative opening prayers.

9. DOL 123:880.

began to be used by the churches of the English-speaking world on the First Sunday of Advent in 1974.

PREPARING FOR A REVISION OF THE SACRAMENTARY
Even before the project of revising all the ICEL books formally began in 1981, the Advisory Committee was already discussing the Sacramentary under such topics as the nature of an opening prayer, the composition of new texts for a pilot project dealing with prayers over the gifts and prayers after Communion, and the possibility of composing new Eucharistic Prayers.[10] At the 1981 meeting of the Advisory Committee a paper on "The Nature and Function of Liturgical Language: One Perspective" by Kathleen Hughes, R.S.C.J., generated a good deal of discussion.[11] A related topic was an extended discussion of the desirability of relating newly composed opening prayers of the Mass to the Scripture readings of the day. New French versions of the opening prayers took their inspiration from the gospel and the Advisory Committee was trying to decide whether or not to move in this direction. One member noted that if such a relationship were to be decided upon, prayers would be needed for the three cycles, and that this would be "a monumental task."[12] Eventually, a resolution was passed "that ICEL commission the preparation of a set of new opening prayers for the major seasons of the liturgical year and the Sundays of Ordinary Time (C Cycle) inspired by and reflecting the content of the assigned scripture readings and especially the gospel texts."[13] At that same meeting decisions were made to commission the preparation of a corpus of new prayers over the gifts and prayers after Communion and to prepare a consultation for the revision of the Sacramentary.

At its 1982 meeting in Rome, the Advisory Committee took two further steps that were significant for the work of composing new prayers in English. A resolution was passed to form a new Original Texts Subcommittee which would operate as an experiment until the next Advisory Committee meeting. Previously, the task of composing

10. Minutes of Advisory Committee Meeting [hereafter AC Minutes], May 19–23, 1980, ICEL Archives.

11. This was revised as an ICEL occasional paper and entitled *The Language of Liturgy: Some Theoretical and Practical Implications* (Washington, D.C.: ICEL, 1982).

12. The speaker was Rev. Frederick McManus. See AC Minutes, June 8–12, 1981, p. 17, ICEL Archives.

13. Ibid., 35.

original texts had been part of the work of the subcommittee for Translations, Revisions, and Original Texts (TROT). In addition to lessening the large workload of this subcommittee, this move was also a recognition that the composition of new prayers required different skills from the work of translation and revision.[14] The following resolution was also passed.

"Be it resolved that a book of newly composed presidential prayers covering the period 4 September 1983 to 25 December 1983 be prepared. This book would contain opening prayers for Sundays and Solemnities inspired by the Scripture readings of the day, particularly but not exclusively by the Gospel. It would also contain a smaller sampling of seasonal prayers over the gifts and prayers after communion. It is foreseen that trial use of these prayers by various communities in the ICEL member and associate member countries will give sufficient information to determine the feasibility of the preparation of a three year cycle of opening prayers and a collection of about twenty (20) Prayers Over the Gifts and about twenty (20) Prayers After Communion."[15]

The results of this consultation were discussed at the 1984 meeting of the Advisory Committee and at the joint meeting of the Advisory Committee and Episcopal Board that followed. Kathleen Hughes, chair of the subcommittee on Original Texts, reported that the overall response to the prayers had been positive and that consultants had often identified the relationship to Scripture, the fresh language, and the concrete, existential character of the texts as strengths.[16] Some of the prayers were criticized for containing too many themes and occasionally attempting to sermonize. There was also some concern in the discussions about the durability of these new prayers. It was agreed that the project of new presidential prayers would go forward but, at this point, the Advisory Committee was still undecided about the number of new presidential prayers that would be included in the revised Sacramentary. It would be at the August 1985 meeting of the Advisory Committee that decisions would be made about what additions would be made to the 1973 Sacramentary. These decisions

14. AC Minutes, November 2–6, 1982, ICEL Archives. For the discussion see p. 14; for the resolution see p. 30. This subcommittee would become one of ICEL's regular working groups.

15. Ibid., 30.

16. AC Minutes, August 21–25, 1984, p. 6, ICEL Archives.

were made on the basis of data drawn from widespread consultation. The additional material was to include, among other things, three cycles of opening prayers for all Sundays and a collection of prayers over the gifts and prayers after Communion.[17]

THE PROCESS OF PROVIDING NEW PRAYERS

How does an international commission go about the process of composing new prayers for the Church? The first task was that of finding authors and this was not easy. Of the forty names that had been suggested at a 1982 Advisory Committee meeting only a handful had demonstrated an ability to do the work.[18] In 1985 the Original Texts Subcommittee discussed original opening prayers submitted by fifteen authors in order to decide which authors would be asked to continue with the project. A team of three (Team A) was chosen to work on opening prayers and a second team of three (Team B) was chosen to work on other original texts planned as part of the revision.[19]

"Whose prayer is it and who does any necessary revisions? These questions had to be resolved early on and, at a 1985 meeting of the subcommittee on Original Texts, the following process was outlined to guide ICEL's relationship with its authors.

1. Once an author submitted a text, an initial stipend was to be given, signifying ICEL's ownership of the text.
2. The subcommittee would work on minor problems detected in the text until satisfied.
3. A text judged largely unacceptable was to be sent back to the author for a second try along with the subcommittee's comments.
4. The subcommittee and the authors would occasionally meet together."[20]

At this same meeting the subcommittee reviewed the projected list of original texts proposed for the revision and assigned them to various authors. The texts fell under the following categories: opening

17. For the list see Appendix 2 of the AC Minutes, August 25–29, 1985, ICEL Archives. Some of the decisions made at this meeting would be revised at subsequent meetings.

18. Kathleen Hughes mentioned this in her report to the Episcopal Board at a joint meeting of the Episcopal Board and the Advisory Committee. See EB/AC Minutes, August 26–28, 1984, p. 3, ICEL Archives.

19. Original Texts [hereafter OT] Minutes, August 21–23, 1985, p. 1, ICEL Archives.

20. OT Minutes, December 14–18, 1985, pp. 1–2, ICEL Archives.

prayers for Sundays and Solemnities, prayers for the Chrism Mass, texts for the Order of Mass which included a selection of prefaces and several eucharistic prayers for use with existing prefaces, a collection of weekday collects, prayers over the gifts, prayers after Communion, solemn blessings, prayers for selected ritual Masses, and prayers for various needs and occasions.[21]

A process also had to be worked out to clarify the Advisory Committee's role in the creation of these new texts. In 1987 the steps set out above were refined and others were added. Authors were to be commissioned and their texts submitted to the subcommittee. After the subcommittee discussed the texts further work would be done, as necessary, by the author, if major work was needed, or by an editorial committee, if minor work was needed. Texts would be resubmitted to the subcommittee which would make any further revisions deemed necessary and then submit the texts for discussion at an Advisory Committee meeting. The texts would be returned to the subcommittee with the Advisory Committee's comments and the subcommittee and/or editorial committee would rework the text. Once the text was approved by the subcommittee it would be submitted by mail to the Advisory Committee for a vote. Texts rejected by the Advisory Committee would be returned to the subcommittee which would decide whether to give them to the editorial committee or to commission a new author. Once approved anew by the subcommittee, these texts were to be resubmitted to the Advisory Committee for its vote.[22]

GUIDELINES FOR THE COMPOSITION OF NEW TEXTS
What guidelines could be given to direct the authors of original texts? This was a significant question and had been a matter of discussion for several years. A list of guidelines was composed when the work of composing original prayers was still under the subcommittee on Translations, Revisions, and Original Texts. These would be revised

21. Ibid. For the complete list see Appendix 2 of the minutes. Three new Eucharistic Prayers were prepared during the process but they remain in a file. The first one, known as Eucharistic Prayer A, was approved by eight conferences of bishops but Rome did not confirm their decisions.

22. OT Minutes, December 12–15, 1987, p. 3, ICEL Archives. Of course, once the texts were approved by the Advisory Committee they would be sent to the Episcopal Board for its vote. At a 1988 meeting of the Advisory Committee members of the subcommittee on Original Texts suggested that the Advisory Committee should review the original prayers at least twice before voting on them. See AC Minutes, May 1–4, 1988, p. 3, ICEL Archives.

and supplemented by the subcommittee on Original Texts as it carried out its work. Twenty-four guidelines soon emerged and they were arranged under three headings. Since they were so important to the process I will list them all here.[23]

Function and Structure

1. The author should keep in mind the function of the prayer, its place and purpose in the rite.
2. The prayers are intended for *proclamation* in the liturgical assembly.
3. While the traditional elements of a particular genre of prayer (e.g., the classic order of a collect contains address, amplifications of address, petitions, result clause, conclusion) should be contained in the newly composed prayers, they need not in every instance follow exactly the structure of the prayers now in the Sacramentary or other ritual books.
4. The thoughts expressed in the prayers should have a logical coherence and unity and the prayers should have a coherent structure.
5. The nature of the rite as well as the moment in the rite and its ritual context will influence the tone of the prayer.

Content and Style

6. The prayers must be doctrinally sound.
7. Inspiration for the prayers will be found in the Scriptures, the seasons, and the theology underlying the various rites. For example, references to baptism would be expected in some presidential prayers in Lent and the Easter season.
8. The prayers should have enough substance to draw the congregation into prayer and to afford inspiration for meditation.
9. The themes of the prayers should be fairly universal so that they can be used in a variety of places and circumstances. In addition, these compositions are prepared for an international community and should avoid themes that might be suitable for a particular community or region but would be meaningless or confusing in other circumstances.
10. As far as possible the author should avoid moving from the concrete to the abstract in prayer composition. A concrete prayer is one that is rooted in human experience and speaks of basic

23. The list is taken from Appendix 1 of OT Minutes, December 14–18, 1985, ICEL Archives. For a helpful commentary on these guidelines see H. Kathleen Hughes, "Original Texts: Beginnings, Present Projects, Guidelines," *Shaping English Liturgy,* 242–54.

human concerns. Thus rooted in human experience, a prayer can be concrete and universal at the same time.

11. The compositions should be clear, forceful, interesting, consistent, and imaginative.

12. There should be a consistency of images, and care must be exercised not to use too many images in a single prayer, lest the hearers become confused.

13. An effort should be made to open the prayers to a wide ranging vocabulary. Color and poetic imagery, where possible, should be evident in the compositions. At the same time jargon or esoteric words should be avoided.

14. The prayers should use inclusive language and avoid the use of language which may discriminate on sexist, racist, clericalist, or anti-Semitic grounds.

15. Attention to rhythm and cadence must be a primary consideration in the composition of new prayers.

16. Prayers should be composed in sense lines, this with a view to their being proclaimed well, heard, and easily understood.

17. Authors should avoid stock-in-trade collect phrases.

18. Original texts should in general be fuller than the corresponding ICEL translations.

Trinitarian Concerns

19. Christian liturgical prayer is traditionally directed to the Father, through the mediation of the Son, in the power of the Spirit.

20. Care must be taken to respect the Trinitarian economy. Traditional titles ordinarily ascribed to the Father are not used of the Son or the Spirit.

21. Within the prayers references to the different persons of the Trinity must be expressed clearly, especially when pronouns (e.g., you, he) are being used.

22. Presidential prayers should be addressed to the First Person of the Trinity. This may be done in a variety of ways and authors are encouraged to incorporate a wide range of metaphors, especially those drawn from the Scriptures, in the forms of address of the prayers. The choice of address should be made bearing in mind the content of the balance of the prayer.

23. While presidential prayers are traditionally addressed to the First Person of the Trinity, there are other genre (e.g., litanies) which may be addressed to the Son or the Spirit.

24. Attention must be given to the conclusions of the prayers in order that they express the mediation of Christ. The conclusion, whether standard or more inventive, should fit together with what has gone before in the body of the prayers. It may be interwoven within the prayer. If there is a doxology in the body of the prayer, it seems best to omit a full doxology in the conclusion.

These criteria are obviously in accord with the stipulation set out at Vatican II that any new forms adopted in the liturgy should grow organically from already existing forms (SC 23). While the use of the Scriptures as a source of inspiration is something new in these prayers and richer imagery is to be expected, it is clear that the traditional structure of a collect is to serve as a guiding form from which new prayers are to organically grow. It is also clear that departures from the Trinitarian theology evident in traditional Christian prayers would not be welcome.

It was at the 1985 meeting of the subcommittee on Original Texts that this version of the guidelines was established and, at that same meeting, a discussion took place between the subcommittee and the authors of team A who were working on the Scripture-related opening prayers for the revised Missal. Further directions to guide the authors emerged in this discussion. They were urged to be careful to make sure "that the new opening prayers are prayers and not a didactic prelude to the readings."[24] In accord with the second guideline which called attention to the proclamatory nature of the prayers, the authors were asked to read them aloud when they were composing them. At each stage of review, whether subcommittee, Advisory Committee, or joint meetings of the Episcopal Board and Advisory Committee, the prayers would also be read aloud. This turned out to be a significant practice because certain characteristics or qualities of the prayers became evident in the proclaiming or the hearing that could easily be overlooked by a mere reading. The assembly's familiarity with the classic structure and order of a collect was given as a reason for maintaining this structure in the bulk of the new prayers.

SCRIPTURE-RELATED OPENING PRAYERS

The task of composing three sets of Scripture-related opening prayers for Sundays and Solemnities was a daunting one. Many questions would emerge in the process and issues would have to be addressed

24. OT Minutes, December 14–18, 1985, p. 2, ICEL Archives.

and resolved. For example, while there was agreement that the gospel of the day would provide the chief inspiration for the new prayers, authors also had to take into account the liturgical feast or season which provided the context within which this gospel was proclaimed.[25] While imagery from the gospel could appear in the prayers, the authors could not presume familiarity with the gospel passage on the part of the hearers. Prayers would also be criticized if the scriptural imagery employed in the prayer was too literal. At one meeting the subcommittee rejected a proposed prayer because it concentrated on a secondary aspect of the gospel and missed the central focus. Another was accepted because it was concise, had good rhythm, and benefited from a single controlling image. A third was sent back to the author for revision because "this prayer gave an intellectual appreciation of the gospel while failing to use the simple and more concrete imagery that the gospel provides."[26]

Sometimes prayers were rejected because "they did not represent a new stage of development such as the subcommittee hoped for in new presidential prayers. The language and style of the texts were not sufficiently original."[27] The question of just how original an original prayer was supposed to be was a matter of ongoing discussion. At one point a question arose in the Advisory Committee about whether it was realistic or legitimate to expect that these new prayers would be the fruit of prayer. The context was a criticism by some people that certain prayers "seemed to lack prayerfulness and the effort at composing them was looked upon as more of a literary exercise." This generated an interesting discussion in which several members argued that the prayers had to be broad and general enough in order to be the prayer of a liturgical assembly, and one person suggested that the prayerfulness of a prayer proclaimed in public was dependent on the prayerfulness of those who were praying it.[28]

In October of 1986 ICEL issued another consultation booklet which was entitled *Opening Prayers for Experimental Use at Mass*. The collection of twenty-two prayers included opening prayers for the Church's

25. Just how concrete the connection with the feast or season should be was a matter of disagreement. For a discussion about whether or not the alternative opening prayer for the First Sunday of Lent (A Cycle) should include a reference to the elect see AC Minutes, October 24–28, 1991, p. 40, ICEL Archives.
26. OT Minutes, June 17-20, 1988, pp. 3–4, ICEL Archives.
27. OT Minutes, August 25–28, 1986, p. 6, ICEL Archives.
28. AC Minutes, September 3–6, 1987, p. 20, ICEL Archives.

major celebrations from the First Sunday of Advent to the Eighth Sunday in Ordinary Time (A Cycle). The purpose was "to provide the several authors of the new opening prayers and ICEL's subcommittee on original texts, which is overseeing their work, with further response and direction as they carry forward the present phase of the project."[29] The intent was to present the prayers for actual use in liturgical assemblies so that responses would be based on the experience of their proclamation in the liturgy. A brief questionnaire accompanied the collection. Respondents were asked to indicate which of the prayers were used in the liturgical assembly and to use the following categories in evaluating each prayer: content, structure, style, suitability for proclamation, and intelligibility for those hearing them. A third question asked if the prayers contained "successful echoes of or allusions to the Scripture readings of the day, particularly the gospel reading."[30] Respondents were also invited to make additional comments.

A look at the prayer for the First Sunday of Advent along with some of the comments from the consultation will illustrate something of the process and criteria at work. The following version appeared in the consultation booklet.

"Let us pray.
Pause for silent prayer.
Above the clamor of our violence
your Word of truth resounds,
O God of majesty and power.
Over nations enshrouded in despair
Your justice dawns.

Grant your household
a discerning spirit and a watchful eye
to perceive the hour in which we live.
Hasten the advent of that Day
when the weapons of war shall be banished,
our deeds of darkness cast off,
and all your scattered children gathered into one.

We ask this through him whose coming is certain,
whose Day draws near:

29. *Opening Prayers for Experimental Use at Mass* (Washington, D.C.: ICEL, 1986) 6.
    30. Ibid., 7.

88

your Son, our Lord Jesus Christ,
who lives and reigns with you and the Holy Spirit,
one God, for ever and ever."[31]

While there was appreciation of biblical allusions in the favorable
comments on the prayer, some thought that there were too many
powerful images and the word "enshrouded" was deemed problematic. A number commented on the odd structure of the prayer in
which God was not addressed until the third line. This was one of
several prayers in the booklet which employed such an attempt at
originality in the structure of an opening prayer. All would eventually be revised to restore the address to the very beginning of the
prayer.[32] The conclusion of the prayer received strong affirmation.
The final revision of this prayer is as follows:

"God of majesty and power,
amid the clamor of our violence
your Word of truth resounds;
upon a world made dark by sin
the Sun of Justice casts his dawning rays.

Keep your household watchful
and aware of the hour in which we live.
Hasten the advent of that day
when the sounds of war will be for ever stilled,
the darkness of evil scattered,
and all your children gathered into one.

We ask this through him whose coming is certain,
whose day draws near:
your Son, our Lord Jesus Christ,
who lives and reigns with you in the unity of the Holy Spirit,
God for ever and ever."[33]

All four prayers for the Sundays of Advent have the same conclusion. The subcommittee encouraged authors to compose one conclusion

31. Ibid., 10.
32. While this original structure did not survive in these prayers, the revised Sacramentary does include some prayers which do not begin with an
address to God. For example, the alternative opening prayer of the Second
Sunday of Advent (Year B) begins as follows: "With tender comfort and trans-
forming power you come into our midst, O God of mercy and might."
33. *The Sacramentary*, vol. 1 (Washington, D.C.: ICEL, 1998) 180.

for each season for they thought that this would be "a subtle way of expressing the liturgical unity of the season."[34] This practice received a favorable response in the consultation and appears in the revised Sacramentary. Most of the original opening prayers for the season of Christmas end in the following manner.

"We ask this through Jesus Christ, your Word made flesh,
who lives and reigns with you in the unity of the Holy Spirit,
in the splendor of eternal light,
God for ever and ever."

The alternative opening prayers of the season of Lent often end in the following manner.

"Grant this through Christ, our liberator from sin,
who lives and reigns with you in the unity of the Holy Spirit,
holy and mighty God for ever and ever."

On a number of Sundays in Lent the first line of this conclusion is changed to read "We ask this through Christ, our deliverance and hope." Almost all of the prayers of the Easter season employ one of the following conclusions.

"Grant this through Jesus Christ, the resurrection and the life,
who lives and reigns with you in the unity of the Holy Spirit,
God for ever and ever."

"Grant this through Jesus Christ, the firstborn from the dead,
who lives and reigns with you now and always
in the unity of the Holy Spirit,
God for ever and ever."[35]

In accord with the twenty-second guideline, authors were encouraged to incorporate a wide range of metaphors when addressing God in the Scripture-related opening prayers. The 1986 consultation book-

34. Hughes, "Original Texts: Beginnings, Present Projects, Guidelines," p. 254, n. 49. When the subcommittee agreed that a single doxology should be used for each of the major seasons this was not meant to deter the authors from composing doxologies integrated into the body of the prayer, particularly for those in Ordinary Time. See OT Minutes, June 14–18, 1989, p. 9, ICEL Archives.

35. The Lenten and Easter doxologies were finally the work of an editorial committee of the subcommittee. The choice of which alternative to use was based on whether or not a prayer ended with a reference to Christ. See OT Minutes, January 29–February 2, 1992, p. 1, ICEL Archives.

let included such forms of address as "God of glory and splendor," "Good and gracious God," "God our Creator," "Most High God," "Lord God of the nations," "God of the covenant," "Merciful Father," "God of light and life." While this variety was well received in the consultation, a concern was expressed that arbitrary titles for God should be avoided. In a meeting with the authors, the subcommittee reminded them that the titles used for God should have some relation to the body of the prayer, particularly the petition.[36]

PRAYERS OVER THE GIFTS
AND PRAYERS AFTER COMMUNION

Just as the task of composing alternative opening prayers evoked much discussion about the nature of such a prayer, so too, the decision to compose a selection of original prayers over the gifts and prayers after Communion was accompanied by ongoing discussion about the nature and function of these prayers.[37] In 1981 the Advisory Committee decided to commission twenty sets of prayers over the gifts and prayers after Communion. There would be two for Advent, two for Christmas, three for Lent, three for Easter, and ten for Ordinary Time. The intent was that "as common texts for a season, these prayers would have more of a seasonal flavor and would not have to be related to the scriptural readings of a particular Sunday."[38] In 1985 the number of proposed new texts was changed and there was some discussion of the possibility of relating the new prayers after Communion to the gospel of the day or the gospels within a particular season.[39] The revised Sacramentary actually contains fourteen newly composed prayers over the gifts: two each for the weekdays of Advent, Christmas, Lent, and Easter, and six for Ordinary Time. There are nineteen new prayers after Communion for weekday Masses: three for Advent, two for Christmas, six for Lent, three for Easter, and five for Ordinary Time.

36. For this and other recommendations from the subcommittee see OT Minutes, June 3–6, 1987, pp. 4–6, ICEL Archives.

37. See AC Minutes, June 8–12, 1981, pp. 8–9, ICEL Archives, for some discussion of what should go into a brief which would be sent to authors commissioned to compose these prayers.

38. Ibid., p. 17. For the resolution see p. 35.

39. See AC Minutes, August 25–29, 1985, p. 19 and Appendix 2, ICEL Archives. Inspiration for the suggestion that the prayers after Communion be related to the gospel readings came from the Italian Missal which followed this practice in the texts of Communion antiphons.

One of the issues that arose in composing prayers over the gifts was whether and how the language of offering should be used. One author's new compositions were criticized for having too great a sense of offering. Another author was asked to compose a couple of new prayers "whose content will make these texts serve more evidently as a *bridge* text between the setting of the table and the great thanksgiving."[40] The following example of an original prayer for the Easter season provides an example of such a bridge.

"Living God,
the wheat and vine which spring from the earth
tell of the One you brought from death to life.
Look upon these gifts of bread and wine
and receive with them
the praise of a people
you have raised to new life.
Grant this through Jesus Christ our Lord."[41]

What was to be original in the new prayers after Communion? In one of the subcommittee meetings the suggestion was made that the originality would appear in the petition. A proposal was made that it should be slightly longer than those in the present Roman prayers, that it employ concrete imagery which might be drawn from the Scriptures of a season, and finally, that it should pray "for the effectiveness of the Eucharist in our lives, for the sake of the community and the world."[42] The following example of an original prayer for the Easter season employs a biblical allusion to lead to the desired mission orientation.

"Loving God,
as the first witnesses of the resurrection
you chose the devoted women
whose service of the Lord Jesus
led them to the tomb.
By this communion in the risen Lord
keep us steadfast in service,

40. OT Minutes, December 13–16, 1988, pp. 12–13, ICEL Archives.
41. *The Sacramentary*, vol. 2 (Washington, D.C.: ICEL, 1988) 177.
42. OT Minutes, December 12–15, 1987, p. 13, ICEL Archives. The point was made by Rev. Edward Matthews who served as chair of the subcommittee on Original Texts at the time.

that we also may have the joy of being his witnesses.
Grant this through Jesus Christ our Lord."[43]

PRAYERS FOR VARIOUS NEEDS AND OCCASIONS
In response to recommendations made during the consultation with
conferences of bishops, ICEL decided to supplement the section of
the sacramentary entitled "Masses and Prayers for Various Needs
and Occasions" with some new prayers. A tentative list of occasions
which needed new prayers was drawn up in 1985.[44] This would be
modified as the subcommittee on Translations and Revisions identified current prayers which need an alternative prayer, as the subcommittee on Original Texts proceeded with its work, and as the
Advisory Committee reviewed the newly composed prayers. A discussion in 1992 revealed some of the difficulties encountered in carrying out this task. It was not easy to find appropriate language for
these prayers, language that was prayerful yet connected to contemporary needs and occasions. Some prayers were too general and did
not have the strength and urgency called for by a particular situation.
A prayer for use in time of industrial conflict was criticized for lacking sufficient prayer language. Another intended for the communications media was rejected because it seemed "too far removed from
the reality of the contemporary communications media," and "to
present too rosy a picture of its operations and aspirations."[45] Work
on the project continued and the revised Sacramentary contains
forty-one newly composed prayers in this section. Most are opening
prayers but there are three sets which contain an opening prayer, a
prayer over the gifts, and a prayer after Communion.

The new prayers respond to a variety of possible situations and
needs. For example, there are prayers for people on pilgrimage, for
those who make their living on the sea, for those who work in indus-
try, commerce, and technology, for victims of violence, for the homeless, the unemployed, the elderly, for young people. The following
prayer composed for victims of abuse will give a sample of what is
available in this section of the book.

"O God,
in whose enduring love we trust,

43. *The Sacramentary*, vol. 2, 177.
44. See AC Minutes, August 25–29, 1985, Appendix 2, ICEL Archives.
45. AC Minutes, September 7–11, 1992, pp. 10–13, ICEL Archives.

bind up the wounds of those betrayed
by abuse at the hands of others.
Heal them and make them whole,
that they may once more receive and give love
with confidence in their dignity as your sons and daughters.

We ask this through our Lord Jesus Christ, your Son,
who lives and reigns with you in the unity of the Holy Spirit,
God for ever and ever."[46]

ALTERNATIVE EASTER PROCLAMATION

Limitations of space do not permit a discussion of all the categories
of newly composed prayers in the revised Sacramentary.[47] However,
mention must be made of the alternative Easter Proclamation or *Ex-sultet* which is a fine example of an original composition. Here poetry
and prayer are woven together as all of creation is invited to rejoice,
and the Church gives praise to God. During the proclamation the
people respond with the following acclamations: "We praise you,
God of everlasting light" and "Now is Christ risen! We are raised
with him!" The opening stanzas offer a taste of what will be found in
the complete text.

"Exult and sing, O shining angel choirs!
Exult and dance, bright stars and blazing suns!
The firstborn of creation, Jesus Christ,
is ris'n in radiant splendor from the dead!

Rejoice, O awesome night of our rebirth!
Rejoice, O mother moon, that marks the months!
For from your fullness comes, at last, the Day
when sin is robbed of pow'r and death is slain!

Awaken, earth! Awaken, air and fire!
O children born of clay and water, come!
The One who made you rises like the sun
to scatter night and wipe your tears away.

Arise then, sleepers, Christ enlightens you!
Arise from doubt and sadness, sin and death.

46. *The Sacramentary*, vol. 2, 1097.
47. For example, the Order of Mass includes a new blessing of water, six
new prefaces, three new acclamations for the Eucharistic Prayer, five new
solemn blessings, and two new prayers over the people.

With joyful hearts and spirits set afire
draw near to sing this Easter candle's praise!"[48]

AN ONGOING SERIES OF NEGOTIATIONS

At the beginning of this article I suggested that the composition of
new prayers for the revised Sacramentary can be understood as another step in the process of the self-actualization of a world Church.
The process of becoming a world Church is a passage from one ecclesial reality to another, and Roland Delattre has identified ritual as a
means by which "we negotiate the terms or conditions for our presence among, and our participation in, the plurality of realities
through which our humanity makes its passage."[49] All kinds of rela-
tionships are negotiated in ritual and the story of the process of including newly composed prayers for the revised Sacramentary is one
which was filled with negotiations. They took place within the Advisory Committee, between that committee and the Episcopal Board,
between authors and the subcommittee on Original Texts, between
the subcommittee and the Advisory Committee, between those consulted and the various committees, between ICEL and the bishops'
conferences, and within the bishops' conferences themselves. In decisions made about the structure and content of the new prayers there
was an implicit negotiation taking place with the Church's tradition
of prayer. Since Italian, French, and German liturgical books were
consulted in the process of composing new English prayers, there
was also some ecclesial reciprocity at work.

The collection of original prayers that enriches the revised Sacramentary is the outcome of rigorous negotiation. One of the concerns
articulated early on in the process of composing original texts was
whether or not they would stand up over the course of time. This will
only be answered as the Church prays these prayers and one more negotiation must take place before the English-speaking churches begin
to pray them. Bishops' conferences of English-speaking churches
throughout the world have submitted the Sacramentary to the Congregation for Worship and the Discipline of the Sacraments for the
confirmatio. Once that is given we will begin the final negotiation, that
which will take place between the prayers and the People of God.

48. *The Sacramentary*, vol. 1, 336.
49. Roland A. Delattre, "Ritual Resourcefulness and Cultural Pluralism,"
Soundings 61 (1978) 282.

Dominic E. Serra

The Greeting of Peace in the
Revised Sacramentary: A New Pastoral Option

The Roman Rite is used by so large a number of Christians the world over that it is difficult to think of it as idiosyncratic or peculiar, but it does exhibit elements that are found in no other ritual family. The placement of the greeting of peace just before Communion rather than before the Eucharistic Prayer is one such peculiarity. In recent years, some have questioned the wisdom of this arrangement. This questioning has raised the possibility that the proposed revision of the "Order of Mass" will allow the option of exchanging the greeting of peace before the anaphora. While it is true that some options are valuable simply because of the variety they allow, it is always a good idea to examine their theological meaning and pastoral implications before making the choice. The elucidation of such implications is precisely the intention of this paper, but first it will be necessary to establish a general context for our discussion and to look at some historical facts and ritual matters.

ECCLESIAL PEACE AND THE LORD'S SUPPER

For two millennia Christians have obeyed the Lord's command to observe a ritual meal in his memory. His promise assures us that the memorial of Christ transforms our ritual supper of bread and wine into the wedding banquet of the Lamb. The command is clear, the object of memorial is obvious, and the essential elements of the meal are unmistakable. There is, however, a component of the command that can escape our attention just as it eluded the Corinthian Christians so many years ago. Paul chided them, saying, "When you come together, it is not really to eat the Lord's supper. For when the time comes to eat, each of you goes ahead with your own supper, and one goes hungry and another becomes drunk" (1 Cor 11:21). It is easy enough for us to recognize the necessity of bread and wine and the importance of eating and drinking them in the Lord's memory, for we believe these elements and actions constitute the very sacramental sign of the eucharistic banquet. For all their importance, however, Paul did not judge them sufficient. Eating and drinking in the Lord's memory is a cause of condemnation for those who do so without attention to the bond of charity. We might say that the charity binding the assembly together in ecclesial peace is also part of the "sacramental sign" of the Lord's Supper, or at least, that such peace generates the essential situation in which the sacramental elements and actions achieve their end.

Surely, Paul was not concerned about canonical validity and liceity when he declared the Corinthian suppers to be other than the Lord's. He was concerned with fidelity to the Savior's command and with the necessity of being true to our identity in Christ lest everything we do be a sham. Pressed too far, this biblical condemnation may cause some to fear that every ill feeling, every judgmental thought, and every social negligence will render our Eucharists ineffective. Pressed not at all, we could be in yet more serious trouble. At least the attitude of love and the desire to be bound to one another in Christ must be present, or our supper could end up being only ours and not the Lord's.[1]

The bond of charity, or ecclesial peace, is at once a prerequisite for the Eucharist and the fruit of its celebration. This is not a paradoxical conundrum. It rather results from the reality that the Church is a mystery born from the very Eucharist of which it is the celebrant, finding in its celebration both the source and the summit of its every activity.[2] This understanding of the Church's relationship to the Eucharist is the context within which we shall discuss the meaning of the greeting of peace and the criterion against which to measure the pastoral options for its observance.

THE GREETING OF PEACE IN THE EARLY CHURCH AT ROME
Immediately after their baptism, Hippolytus tells us, the neophytes are sealed with oil and kissed by the bishop. He adds,

1. See a fuller discussion of these ideas in J. Murphy-O'Connor, "Eucharist and Community in First Corinthians," *Living Bread, Saving Cup* (Collegeville: The Liturgical Press, 1987) 1–29.
2. *Lumen gentium* 11.

"And then they shall pray together with all the people: they do not pray with the faithful until they have carried out all these things. And when they have prayed, they shall give the kiss of peace. And then the offering shall be presented by the deacons to the bishop."[3]

Most scholars believe that such a kiss was exchanged by the faithful of Hippolytus's community every time they gathered to do what the Lord commands. The kiss is initiated by the bishop, assuring the neophytes that the baptismal bath and chrismation join them to the communion of the faithful, that is, to the Eucharist. It is a kiss all the faithful exchange as their liturgy moves from general intercessions to the memorial offering over the bread and the cup. The kiss announces that this community seeks to be faithful to the Lord's command, not only in the elements and actions, but in their mutual love as well.

Scholars agree that the pattern found in the *Apostolic Tradition* of Hippolytus was the norm not only in his early third-century Rome, but that it had been the Roman practice at least since the middle of the second century. Around the year 150, Justin Martyr gives us a description of the baptismal Eucharist. In his *First Apology*, Justin says that the faithful are joined by the neophytes immediately after baptism, and "when we have ended the prayers, we greet one another with a kiss. Then bread and a cup of water and a cup of mixed wine are brought to him who presides. . . ."[4] Justin joins Hippolytus in affirming, that in these early days, the eucharistic offering of the Roman church was preceded by intercessions and the kiss of peace.[5]

3. *Apostolic Tradition* 21. This translation is from Geoffrey J. Cuming, *Hippolytus: A Text for Students* (Bramcote: Grove Books, 1976) 21. The gesture we call "the greeting of peace" was a kiss on the mouth in these early days. For this reason I use the term "kiss" when discussing the ancient and classical form of the greeting.

4. Justin Martyr, *Apologia I*, 65 (PG 6:428). This translation is from R.C.D. Jasper and G. J. Cuming, eds., *Prayers of the Eucharist: Early and Reformed* (New York: Pueblo, 1987) 28.

5. It must be noted that our only witnesses to a pre-anaphoral kiss of peace in Rome are two descriptions of baptismal Eucharists, and further that the Roman Sacramentary evidence is unanimous in excluding the post-anaphoral kiss at the paschal vigil. Is it possible that Rome practiced a post-anaphoral kiss from the beginning except when the Eucharist followed baptism as at the paschal vigil? On such occasions, the entrance of the neophytes into the community and their being sealed and kissed by the bishop before the intercessions may have attracted the kiss of peace to a position following these intercessions as Hippolytus and Justin suggest. There is not nearly enough

The practice of Christians in the eastern part of the empire and its border lands echoes that of Rome in regard to the greeting of peace. The *Apostolic Constitutions,* reflecting the liturgical norms of late fourth-century Syria, has the faithful greeting one another after their intercessions and before the eucharistic offering. They do so after the bishop's greeting, "The peace of God be with you all," in response to the deacon's command, "Greet one another with a holy kiss."[6]

The information this document adds to our understanding of the kiss appears in the rites immediately preceding it. In a series of nearly identical actions, four groups of participants in the Liturgy of the Word are called forward individually in turns. Each group is prayed for by the whole assembly in a litany of intercessions, each is the object of the bishop's concluding prayer of blessing, and each is dismissed from the assembly by the deacon. The groups include those preparing for baptism and those whose baptismal innocence has been compromised by grave sin, the penitents. Only when these have been respectfully excused from the assembly by prayer and blessing do the faithful enter into the liturgical action they alone can perform, the eucharistic offering. As they do so, they greet one another with a holy kiss and approach the altar.[7] The kiss not only completes the prayer of the faithful, but it introduces the liturgical action the faithful alone can accomplish in fulfillment of the Lord's command. I have argued elsewhere that this pattern suggests that the kiss is a "missa" functioning as counterpart to the dismissals, reorganizing the remaining assembly and sending them toward the altar for the sacred action that follows.[8]

The *Apostolic Constitutions* tells us that the kiss precedes the eucharistic offering and is exchanged only by true participants in the sacrificial meal. Those whose continued presence could have made them no more than observers had first to be dismissed because the liturgy is not meant merely to be observed. It is an intrinsically participatory

---

evidence for us to answer this question definitively, but these facts do make one a bit less confident about Rome's earliest practice.

6. *Apostolic Constitutions,* VIII:11.8-9. This translation is from W. Jardine Grisbrooke, *The Liturgical Portions of the Apostolic Constitutions: A Text for Students* (Bramcote: Grove Books, 1990) 30.

7. *Apostolic Constitutions,* VIII:6.3–12.3 (Grisbrooke, 22–31).

8. D. E. Serra, "The Kiss of Peace: A Suggestion from the Ritual Structure of the *Missa,*" *Ecclesia Orans* 14 (1997) 79–94.

action, engaged in by the assembly whose ecclesial bond of charity is expressed by the holy kiss.

The Churches of the East have continued to use the kiss in precisely this way up to the present. Once the communion of the faithful became a rarity rather than the norm, they did not abandon the kiss, but some rites restricted it to those whose participation in the sacrifice could be taken for granted, the concelebrating clergy.[9] The reservation of the kiss to the baptized faithful remains constant as does the relationship of the kiss to their offering of the eucharistic sacrifice and to their participating in it by Communion. Its placement before the anaphora allows it to proclaim the identity of the assembly as a church living in the bond of charity, thus capable of fulfilling the Lord's command.

THE GREETING OF PEACE IN LATE ANTIQUE ROME

The apparent universal agreement in practice concerning the peace did not last long. In 416, Pope Innocent I wrote to the bishop of Gubbio in central Italy and insisted that the only proper moment for exchanging the kiss was after the completion of the sacrifice, that is, after the Eucharistic Prayer, which the kiss is meant to complete and seal.[10] At some point during the two hundred years that separate Innocent from Hippolytus, Rome seems to have developed a new practice. Augustine of Hippo also speaks of a post-anaphoral kiss coming at the end of the Lord's Prayer, thus suggesting that North African Christians also exchange the peace just before Communion.[11]

9. Currently in the Byzantine Liturgy of St. John Chrysostom, the kiss is separated from the dismissals and the prayer of the faithful by the great entrance of the gifts and the offertory litany. While it is exchanged only by the clergy, the greeting "Peace to all" is addressed to the whole assembly and the deacon announces to them, "Let us love one another that with one mind we may confess." This translation is from J. Raya and J. de Vinck, *Byzantine Daily Worship* (Allendale and Combermere: Alleluia Press, 1969) 280. In some Oriental Rites, the kiss has become a ritual touching of hands or a similar expression of respect.

10. Innocent I, *Epist. 25,* 1 (PL 20:553): "Pacem igitur asseris confecta mysteria quosdam populis imperare, vel sibi inter se sacerdotes tradere, cum post omnia, quae aperire non debeo, pax sit necessario indicenda, per quam constet populum ad omnia, quae in mysteriis aguntur atque in ecclesia celebrantur, praebuisse consensum, ac finita esse pacis concludentis signaculo demonstrentur."

11. Augustine, *Serm.* 227 (PL 38:1101): After discussing the Lord's Prayer, he says, "Post ipsam dicitur: Pax vobiscum, et osculantur se Christiani in osculo sancto."

Ever since the time of Innocent, and probably for some time before him, the greeting of peace has followed the anaphora and preceded Communion in the liturgy of Rome. As the Roman Rite spread throughout Europe, it brought this custom with it, even supplanting the pre-anaphoral kiss of some Gallican churches. The African church did not survive the fifth-century onslaught of the Vandals. Its demise left the Roman Rite alone of all the Church's ritual families to preserve this practice, and it has done so for at least sixteen hundred years.

On the other hand, what the Roman practice holds in common with all the others is that the greeting of peace maintained its relationship to the baptized faithful, the eucharistic offering, and to Communion. With the disappearance of regular lay Communion, the Western peace, like its counterpart in the East, was retained only among the clergy, since they alone could be counted on to receive Communion.[12] The greeting of peace, in its classical form, presumes full eucharistic participation in offering and receiving.

THE RITUAL CONTEXT
OF THE POST-ANAPHORAL KISS OF PEACE

It is well known that the Lord's Prayer followed the fraction rather than the canon in Roman practice until the time of Gregory the Great, two hundred years after Innocent's letter. Gregory's concern was to move the prayer so that it could be said while the offerings were still on the altar, that is, before they were removed for the purpose of being broken for distribution. He says nothing about the relationship of the kiss of peace to any of these other ritual elements.[13] Thus, in Augustine's North Africa we have the following order: Eucharistic Prayer, Lord's Prayer, kiss of peace, fraction, Communion. The Roman order familiar to Innocent I was: Eucharistic Prayer, kiss of

12. The kiss was retained in the more solemn celebrations at which it was exchanged by the priest, deacon, and subdeacon as a stylized embrace. It did not survive in the more usual form of celebration called "the low Mass." See the fuller discussed in Joseph Jungmann, *The Mass of the Roman Rite: Its Origins and Development*, trans. Francis A. Brunner (New York: Benziger Brothers, 1955) 1:323–27.

13. Gregory the Great, *Epist.* 9, 12 (PL 77:956): "Orationem dominicam id-circo mox post pacem dicimus, quia mos apostolorum fuit ut ad ipsam solummodo orationem oblationis hostiam consecrarent. Et valde mihi inconveniens visum est, ut precem, quam scholasticus quidam composuerat, super oblationem diceremus, et ipsam traditionem, quam Redemptor noster composuit, super eius Corpus et Sanguinem non diceremus."

peace, fraction, Lord's Prayer, Communion; and the post-Gregorian Roman order was: Eucharistic Prayer, Lord's Prayer, kiss of peace, fraction, Communion.

It will be remembered that when Innocent I insisted upon the Roman practice of exchanging the peace after the canon, he said that doing so seals the great prayer. It is, for him, the best way to complete the prayer and to give ritual expression to the "Amen" that proclaims the assent of the assembly.[14] Augustine's North African Christians also exchanged the peace before Communion but not as a seal on the anaphora. Among them the Lord's Prayer intervened between the anaphora and the kiss of peace. One is reminded of Tertullian, who also spoke of the kiss as a means of sealing the prayer of the Church,[15] though it is likely that he had in mind neither the anaphora nor the Lord's Prayer but rather the general intercessions.

Does the idea of the kiss sealing a liturgical prayer have any real place here aside from providing a rhetorical flourish? It is strongly recommended by Innocent, and Tertullian mentions it, but it is not explained theologically even by these capable writers. Gregory the Great seems unconvinced or ignorant of this idea since he moves the Lord's Prayer forward and makes no apology for disrupting the order so emphatically recommended by Innocent. He ignores the issue when he could just as easily have left the peace as seal on the anaphora by placing the Our Father after the kiss and before the fraction.

I believe this would have been unthinkable because the ritual gesture that begins the fraction is the same rite that initiates the greeting. A particle of the bread is broken off (or taken from the *Sancta* or *fermentum* of a previous papal liturgy) and placed into the cup while the presiding bishop or presbyter says to the assembly, "Pax domini sit semper vobiscum."[16] All greet one another with a kiss and then the fraction continues so that Communion may be received. The

14. See n. 9 above.

15. Tertullian, *De oratione* 18, 1 (CCL 1, 267): ". . . osculum pacis, quod est signaculum orationis."

16. *Ordo Romanus I*, 95–107, M. Andrieu, ed., *Les 'Ordines Romani' du haut moyen-age*, 5 vols. (Louvain, 1961–85) 2:98–102. See also *Missale Romanum 1474*, 1023–30, A. Ward and C. Johnson, eds., *Missalis Romani Editio Princeps Mediolani Anno 1474 Prelis Mandata* (Rome: CLV Edizioni Liturgiche, 1996) 181–83. In this second source and in subsequent editions of the *Missale Romanum* published between Trent and Vatican II, the fraction begins during the embolism to the Lord's Prayer and the commingling is accompanied by the greeting "Pax Domini sit semper vobiscum" immediately thereafter.

Roman kiss of peace relates to the canon in the same way that the reception of Communion draws part of its meaning from the assembly's "Amen" to the anaphora. Although Innocent fails to expound its meaning and Gregory ignores the matter, I believe there is reason to think of the kiss not only as the start of Communion but also as a seal on the Eucharistic Prayer. The Roman kiss of peace is at once a pre-Communion ritual and a post-anaphoral action. The placement of the Lord's Prayer immediately after the canon simply makes this less obvious to casual observation.

THEOLOGICAL SIGNIFICANCE
OF THE PRE-ANAPHORAL KISS OF PEACE

When it occurs before the anaphora, the greeting establishes the identity of the community as the body of Christ whose bond is the charity that has its origin in God. This is more than a grouping of people who happen to like one another, more than a gathering of kind and generous people who may or may not know each other very well. This is the assembly of the people whose lives have been joined to Christ's by means of baptism into his paschal mystery, whose destinies have been bound together by their pilgrimage to an everlasting city wherein the wedding banquet of the Lamb is already in progress. These are the people whose love for one another and whose charity toward all has its beginning in the Cross, the very Cross whose meaning has passed over into the Supper as memorial banquet and foretaste of heaven. Only such as these can offer the paschal sacrifice as if it were their own because they have been immersed in it by baptism and live in it by charity. As they approach the act of eucharistic offering, they greet each other, saying "peace," just as the Lord greeted the disciples on the day of resurrection (John 20:19). "This kiss blends souls one with another," says Cyril of Jerusalem,[17] just as it obliterates the separation from God our sins created. Exchanging the peace just before the offering brings to mind the Lord's advice to abandon our gifts at the altar until we have first become reconciled with one another (Matt 5:23-24). The peace born of baptism makes the community, along with bread and wine and paschal memorial, part of the sacramental signing that makes our Eucharist possible.

17. Cyril of Jerusalem, *Myst. Cat.* V, 3. This translation is from F. L. Cross, ed., *St. Cyril of Jerusalem's Lectures on the Christian Sacraments* (Crestwood, N.Y.: St. Vladimir's Seminary Press, 1995) 72.

THEOLOGICAL SIGNIFICANCE
OF THE POST-ANAPHORAL KISS OF PEACE

If it is true that our commitment to love one another and our being bound together by baptism are prerequisites for the Eucharist, then what are we to make of the exchange of peace when it follows the Eucharistic Prayer? Was it an arbitrary and meaningless shift that occurred in Rome between 215 and 416, that places the greeting after the canon thus separating it from the context on which its theology is founded? While one may argue in favor of the pre-anaphoral kiss and its apparent antiquity, it is not possible to say that the Roman practice is as pointless as it is peculiar.

As was noted earlier, the historical evolution of the ritual in the Roman Rite indicates a connection between the kiss and both the anaphora and the fraction. When we consider Innocent's unexplained observation that the kiss is a concluding seal to the canon, we are able to understand that the peace exchanged has its origin in the sacrifice. The peace offered to the apostles after the resurrection in John's Gospel derives from the sacrificial death and resurrection of the Lord. As we see more explicitly laid out in Luke's Gospel, the completion of the paschal mystery in the ascension and pentecostal sending of the Holy Spirit generates the Church, the community of paschal peace. Just so, the anamnesis of the Lord's paschal sacrifice and its being offered in the eucharistic action envelops the participants in the embrace of paschal peace by which they are reconciled to God and joined to one another in the bond of charity (theological charity, that is). Thus, the greeting of peace is an anticipation of the eucharistic Communion and expresses an element of its meaning.

When the bread for the Eucharist was still leavened even in the West and formed into large loaves, the fraction was a practical necessity for the distribution of Communion. This practical action, however, is the sacramental vehicle for proclaiming the communicants to be the one Body of Christ united by the one bread they share. The greeting of peace, the breaking of the bread, and the Communion may be spoken of as a single sacramental action, different moments in the expression of one reality.

There is yet another way in which the peace is related to the eucharistic offering. The Roman Canon is very much concerned with the offering of the sacrifice and with its acceptance by God. It, along with many other such prayers, expresses the idea that the identification of the eucharistic elements with the Body and Blood of Christ derives from the acceptability of the offering. Thus, just before the supper narrative, we find the following prayer in the Roman Canon:

"We beg you, God, to make this offering blessed, dedicated, approved, spiritual, and acceptable, so that it may become for us the Body and Blood of your beloved Son, Our Lord Jesus Christ."[18]

The Canon also states that the sanctifying power of these elements to be received in Communion derives from the acceptance of the offering by God at the altar on high, when it asks:

"Almighty God, we pray that your angel may take this sacrifice to your altar in heaven. Then, as we receive from this altar the sacred body and blood of your Son, let us be filled with every grace and blessing."[19]

The people's "Amen" at the end of the anaphora expresses their participation in this sacrifice and their ratification of its being offered so that the bond of charity expressed in the greeting of peace declares God's acceptance of the sacrifice and seals it. Here we indeed receive "every grace and blessing," as we exchange the greeting of the Risen One and anticipate its fulfillment in the wedding banquet of the Lamb. The kiss is proleptic of the eternal peace of the "sacrum convivium" in the reign of God. The Roman greeting of peace, both ritually and theologically, is a post-anaphoral and pre-Communion ritual.

FURTHER CONSEQUENCES
OF THE THEOLOGICAL OBSERVATIONS
I should like to highlight two consequences of these observations. First, the post-anaphoral greeting, by which the Church declares peace to be the fruit of the Eucharist, preserves us from a quasi-

18. ICEL, *The Sacramentary* (New York: Catholic Book Publishing Co., 1974) 1062: "Quam oblationem tu, Deus, in omnibus quaesumus, benedictam, adscriptam, ratam, rationabilem acceptabilemque facere digneris: ut nobis Corpus et Sanguinis fiat dilectissimi Filii tui, Domini nostri Iesu Christi . . . ." My translation indicates the sense of the Latin in which the acceptability of the offering is related to the transformation of the elements into the Body and Blood of the Lord.

19. *The Sacramentary*, 1063, "Supplices te rogamus, omnipotens Deus: iube haec perferri per manus sancti Angeli tui in sublime altare tuum, in conspectu divinae maiestatis tuae: ut, quotquot ex hac altaris participatione sacrosanctum Filii tui Corpus et Sanguinem sumpserimus, omni benedictione caelesti et gratia repleamur" (English translation, *The Sacramentary*, 546).

Pelagian understanding of the pre-anaphoral greeting. It offers the same corrective to a common misrepresentation of the Roman practice as a solely pre-Communion greeting. Second, the pre-Communion greeting exchanged in conjunction with the fraction emphasizes the communal significance of the Communion rite that remains highly personal and individual in the spiritual imagination of many Catholics of the Roman Rite.

In the first place, one frequently hears the pre-anaphoral greeting defended for its being a statement of a moral imperative. It is spoken of both as an expression of the assembly's unity and as a means of reconciliation. In either case, it is too easily misunderstood to be the cause of our unity or the sign that we have already joined ourselves to one another by our mutual love. The mistaken notion that we are the authors of our peace is not far removed from such ideas.

Viewed in this way, the greeting of peace cleanses us from the sins of hatred, prejudice, hostility, and uncharity. It appears to be a modern form of "going to confession before every Communion." The correct balance between being properly prepared to offer the sacrifice and to receive Communion and its exaggeration in the preconciliar practice is a rather delicate one. While we have nearly abandoned the exaggeration by which sacramental absolution was thought a prerequisite for Communion, we have found comfort in the penitential rite at the start of the liturgy and in this rite of settling our communitarian differences just before offering our gifts or receiving Communion. Attached to this lurks the imagination that our renewed intention to reform is the source of our peace, making us worthy to offer the Eucharist.

Of course, this misunderstanding is also present in our pre-Communion greeting, and I fear it is this instinct that makes the pre-anaphoral greeting so attractive to some as a means of settling our disagreements before offering our gifts at the altar. The idea of the customary Roman greeting as post-anaphoral can rescue us from this exaggeration because it highlights the eucharistic offering as the source of reconciliation and of the prolepsis of eschatological peace. "Becoming what we are"[20] is one way of understanding the Communion rite. Recognizing our true identity as the People of God united by the bond of God's charity makes the greeting both the expression of this reality and the act of our rededication to living in that charity.

---

20. This is a repeated expression of St. Augustine. See Augustine, *Serm.* 272 (PL 38:1247).

The Church's possession of both a pre-anaphoral and a post-anaphoral greeting of peace allows each to contribute to the interpretation of the other. In this case, the pre-anaphoral greeting can be seen to be something far richer than an ethical injunction. As was pointed out earlier, the bond of charity is established by our baptism into the paschal mystery in which we are conformed to the body of Christ and so share in the charity by which the Trinity lives. Joined to Christ's pasch, we are joined to "theological charity" and so become capable of loving our neighbor. It is also a sacramental expression of our being the Church of Christ, capable of offering his paschal sacrifice.

Yes, we must be reconciled to one another before offering our gifts as Christ commands. But such reconciliation is born of the sacrifice we offer. This tension reflects the tension that assures us of theological precision in the discussion of grace and works. Choosing one to the exclusion of the other may produce the consistency that satisfies smaller ways of thinking of the great mysteries, but it will yield neither theological precision nor a spirituality that truly flows from the ritual action of the liturgy. The ritual tension between pre-anaphoral and post-anaphoral greetings and between post-anaphoral and pre-Communion understandings of the Roman practice enrich rather than obfuscate our appreciation of the mystery of our being the Church. The tension is necessary for us to perceive the relationship between Church and Eucharist.

Second, the pre-Communion greeting of peace not only expresses the charity that allows us to receive Communion without suffering Paul's Corinthian condemnation, but it acts as a sacramental sign of the communion created by the paschal sacrifice. The communal dimension of this rite was one of the most challenging lessons to be learned from the liturgical reforms after Vatican II. For a very long time, Catholics of the Roman Rite were taught to think of Communion primarily as an act of receiving the host, that is Jesus Christ. It was a moment of intense personal prayer focusing on the miraculous presence of Christ hidden under the form of bread. The people who happened to be near us were not to be noticed during Communion or while we "made a thanksgiving" after receiving. Such notice could present a distraction at the moment of sacramental union with Jesus. In order to accomplish this sort of singularity of attention to Jesus alone we had to overcome the very experience intended by the sacramental action of eating and drinking in common and we had to reinterpret the word "communion" to mean "union." We rose to the challenge.

The action of receiving Communion in the Roman Rite is now a procession to the Lord's table and an act of eating and drinking that serves as a foretaste of the wedding banquet of the Lamb. No longer is the presence of other worshipers a possible source of distraction, but rather part of the very rite of Communion. Attention to their presence with us in this procession helps us know ourselves as the people whose destinies are joined in the end term of the procession, the banquet in God's Reign. So intense is our union with Christ in this moment that we find ourselves bound to one another in the very love by which the Savior has bound himself to each of us. For the Christian, union with God that is not a communion is merely an illusion.

The liturgy indicates that during this procession the assembly is to sing in order to strengthen the sense of communion.[21] The fact that many parishes have simply abandoned all attempts to encourage the people to sing during Communion may be a symptom of an inability to appreciate the intrinsically communal dimension of this rite. The same may be true of those who believe the greeting of peace is poorly placed in the Roman Rite because it introduces a distracting intermission into the service just when we are about to enter into a moment of intense union with Christ. The idea that the greeting of peace ought to be placed elsewhere in the liturgy because it distracts the participants from the true meaning of Communion is supported neither by our tradition nor by the Roman Rite Eucharistic Liturgy. To move it for this reason would be a mistake and another capitulation to a eucharistic spirituality the conciliar reforms declared to be misguided. The abandonment of the Communion song joined with the abandonment of the greeting of peace for this reason may signal a failure to accept the challenge of the reform to shape our spirituality to the theology expressed in the rubrics and actions of the Church's liturgy.

If the greeting of peace is not connected to the understanding of Communion as foretaste of the heavenly banquet, it may become nothing more than an intermission. Cut loose of its moorings, it could disintegrate into a time for idle chatter and our attention to the sacramental presence of brothers and sisters in communion can become nothing more than silly curiosity about wardrobes and gossip.

21. *General Instruction of the Roman Missal*, 56i (*The Sacramentary*, 27*): "The song during the communion of the priest and people expresses the spiritual union of the communicants who join their voices in a single song, shows the joy of all, and makes the communion procession an act of brotherhood. . . ."

If this is happening, we do not need to move the greeting to a place in the liturgy that may be more suited to these activities; we need to renew the action and deepen its experience in our congregations.

If the Roman Rite is to adopt the option of exchanging the peace before the anaphora it must be done for the reasons indicated earlier in this paper or at least for reasons more noble than the ones just discussed. Its use before the anaphora may help us understand ourselves as the community of God's Church empowered by that grace to celebrate the eucharistic offering. The use of the peace in the baptismal Eucharists of Justin and Hippolytus may suggest that baptismal liturgies are especially apt events for the use of such an option. The theory I have offered elsewhere, that the peace is the mirror image of the dismissal rite,[22] may suggest its use right after the catechumenal dismissals whenever these take place before the anaphora. In this way, the catechumens are identified by the community's prayer for them and by their dismissal and blessing while the faithful and their specific liturgical action is identified by the greeting of peace. As the dismissal sends the catechumens off with a blessing on their advance in faith toward baptism, the greeting sends the faithful to the performance of the Eucharistic Liturgy in which the catechumens will one day join them.

We have examined the greeting of peace, the kiss of ancient liturgies. We have noted its relationship to the context of the communion that is the very meaning of the Lord's Supper. Our historical survey reveals its connections to the anaphora, either as a preparation for it or as a fruit of the offering. We have noted how the pre-anaphoral and post-anaphoral greetings complement each other and enrich the meaning of eucharistic peace. The peace as a Communion ritual highlights the communal dimension of this rite so sorely misunderstood as an exclusively personal encounter with Christ. It is hoped that our examination of these issues puts us in a better position to understand and to catechize about the greeting and to make informed decisions concerning its placement.

22. Serra, 80–83.

Michael G. Witczak

The Eucharistic Prayer in English:
An Analysis and Evaluation of the ICEL Project

INTRODUCTION

Anscar Chupungco, in his book *Liturgies of the Future*,[1] speaks of the adaptation of the Eucharistic Prayer (= EP). He does so in several places with differing emphases. First, he places the EP within the overall structure of the Order of Mass. Since it lies within the liturgy of the Eucharist, it must be adapted to the sacramental character of the Eucharist, namely that it celebrates the dying and rising of Christ using the shape of a ritual meal, as Christ did at the Last Supper.[2]

Moreover, he considers the EP not just as meal prayer within the overall structure of the celebration, but also as a text that needs to be adapted to the culture of the people of the local church. Chupungco very succinctly and pointedly summarizes the outline of the EP as outlined in the General Instruction of the Roman Missal (= GIRM) 55.[3] He also reminds us that even within the EP there is a hierarchy of importance. According the Consilium for the implementation of the Constitution on the Sacred Liturgy, the essentials of the anaphora must be taught to the people. "They consist of a central core and its further elaboration. The core is the narrative-reactualization of what Jesus did at the last supper, leaving out only the breaking of the bread and the communion, which come at the final part of the Mass."[4]

1. Subtitled *The Process and Methods of Inculturation* (New York/Mahwah: Paulist, 1989).

2. Chupungco, 76–77.

3. (Rome, 1969/1970/1974); ET in *Documents on the Liturgy, 1963–1979: Conciliar, Papal, Curial* (Collegeville: The Liturgical Press, 1982) 482–83. Hereafter cited as DOL and page number.

4. Guidelines *Au cours des derniers mois* 2, DOL 615. See Chupungco, 79–80.

The core includes the hymn praising the Father for his gifts, the narrative of Jesus' actions and his words at the Last Supper, supplication to the Father to make the narrative effective, the memorial command, and the doxology. This core is elaborated by the *Sanctus*, the intercessions, and the commemoration of the saints.[5]

The local churches were invited to submit specimens of inculturated EPs to the Consilium (later the Congregation for Divine Worship) for study and approval. Chupungco details three approaches to this kind of inculturation: the Indian bishops' proposal of 1970; the *Missel Romain pour les diocèses du Zaire* of 1988; and the *Misa ng Bayang Filipino* of 1976.[6] The Indian adaptations for the EP involved movement and gesture, adapting the ceremony of the *arati* (using flowers, incense, and light) at the end of the prayer. The Zairean prayer, while it follows the Roman structure outlined in GIRM 55, modifies it to allow participation by the people during the preface, intercessions, and final doxology; it respects the cadences, rhythms, and images of the African language. The Filipino adaptation used idioms and expressions of the Tagalog language to capture the theological truths of the Roman original.

This paper will explore the work of the International Commission on English in the Liturgy (ICEL) as it attempts to inculturate the Roman Rite for the English-speaking world. We will do so in three steps: a basic overview of the passage of the EP from Latin to English; a look at the scholarly background to the understanding of the EP; and a presentation of the texts proposed by ICEL for inclusion in the revised Sacramentary.

THE PASSAGE FROM LATIN TO ENGLISH

By 1966 the decision had been made by Pope Paul VI that the venerable Roman Canon be left intact and that additional EPs should be found or composed.[7] The Consilium's preliminary decisions included adopting a common structure for all the prayers (found now in GIRM 55), creating a variety of literary styles within the structure, choosing to propose three additional prayers, adapting the words of the institution narrative to bring it into closer conformity with the

5. DOL 615; Chupungco, 80.

6. Chupungco, 86–94.

7. The history is detailed by Annibale Bugnini, *The Reform of the Liturgy, 1948–1975*, trans. Matthew J. O'Connell (Collegeville: The Liturgical Press, 1990) 448–87; here, 450.

scriptural and liturgical tradition, inserting an acclamation for the people after the institution narrative, and creating embolisms for use at special sacramental and ritual celebrations.[8]

After some delays, the retouched Roman Canon and the three new EPs along with eight new prefaces were published with norms for their use on 23 May 1968. It was these prayers that then entered the new *Missale Romanum* in 1970. Additional prefaces made a total of eighty-one.[9]

The period of experimentation had led to a number of special EPs, some approved and some not.[10] Eventually, the Congregation for Divine Worship took the initiative and provided EPs for Masses with Children and for Masses of Reconciliation, the latter especially for use in the Holy Year 1975. These five additional prayers appeared on 1 November 1974. Three were for Masses with Children[11] and two for Masses of Reconciliation. Originally approved for use for only three years, the permission was extended first to 1980, and then indefinitely.[12]

Finally, there is the prayer prepared for the Swiss Synod and approved in 1974. It was originally published in German, French, and Italian for use in Switzerland, and was soon approved for use in Luxembourg, France, Germany, Austria, and Italy. Subsequently, translations were made into Spanish and other languages. In 1991 the Congregation for Divine Worship and the Discipline of the Sacraments issued an official version in Latin for the universal Church. The prayer was changed in order to render it theologically consistent with the original four prayers.[13]

ICEL, founded in 1963, is responsible for preparing translations of all liturgical texts for the English-speaking world, and prepared

8. Ibid., 450–56.

9. *Missale Romanum* (Rome: Libreria Editrice Vaticana, 1970, 1975); Bugnini, 396.

10. See Bugnini, *The Reform of the Liturgy,* 465–76.

11. See the studies by Christopher J. Coyne, "The Eucharistic Prayers for Masses with Children: A Theological and Liturgical Analysis," doctoral dissertation (Rome: Pontifical Liturgical Institute, 1994); "Eucharistic Prayers for Masses with Children: Some Observations," *Liturgical Ministry* 4 (Summer 1995) 109–19.

12. Details and citations in Bugnini, *The Reform of the Liturgy,* 482, esp. n. 50.

13. See the discussion in Enrico Mazza, *The Eucharistic Prayers of the Roman Rite* (Collegeville: The Liturgical Press/Pueblo, 1986) 213–18; and Cesare Giraudo, *Preghiere eucaristiche per la chiesa di oggi: Riflessioni in margine al commento del canone svizzero-romano* (Rome: Gregorian University Press, 1993) 19–24.

English versions of each of these prayers.[14] These translations were submitted to the various member conferences of bishops who approved them and submitted them to the Holy See for confirmation. The ICEL version of the eight prefaces and four EPs was approved by the National Conference of Catholic Bishops and confirmed by the Holy See in 1968.[15] It appeared in the *Sacramentary for Sundays and Other Occasions: Provisional Text*[16] and in the final version of *The Sacramentary*.[17] The eighty-one Roman prefaces were expanded by three prefaces expressly for use in the United States of America: one for Thanksgiving Day and two for use on Independence Day or other national holidays.

ICEL's version of the Eucharistic Prayers for Masses with Children and for Masses of Reconciliation were published as a separate booklet in 1975.[18] The prayer of the Swiss Synod, *Eucharistic Prayer for Masses for Various Needs and Occasions,* was published as a separate booklet in 1996.[19]

ICEL's work on EPs was not limited to the preparation of translations of the official Latin prayers. The members of the various committees also prepared auxiliary materials, such as editions of the EP of Hippolytus (1983) and of St. Basil (1985). These two texts were issued for consultation by the conferences of bishops with an eye toward fostering ecumenical liturgical unity.[20] ICEL also produced an original EP in 1984 entitled Eucharistic Prayer A. Though approved by eight episcopal conferences, it was never confirmed by the Holy See.[21]

14. See Frederick R. McManus, "ICEL: The Early Years," *Shaping English Liturgy: Studies in Honor of Archbishop Denis Hurley* (Washington, D.C.: Pastoral Press, 1990) 433–59.

15. See John Page, "ICEL, 1966–1989: Weaving the Words of Our Common Christian Prayer," *Shaping English Liturgy,* 474.

16. Washington, D.C.: NCCB and the Bishops Committee on the Liturgy, 1972.

17. New York: Catholic Book; and Collegeville: The Liturgical Press, 1974.

18. These five prayers were incorporated into an appendix at the end of the 1985 edition of *The Sacramentary.*

19. The prayers issued in Latin in 1991 were completed by ICEL in 1994. It took two years to agree upon the proper format for publishing them in the U.S.

20. *Eucharistic Prayer of Hippolytus: Text for Consultation* (Washington, D.C.: ICEL, 1983); *Eucharistic Prayer of Saint Basil: Text for Consultation* (Washington, D.C.: ICEL, 1985); see Page, 487–88.

21. *An Original Eucharistic Prayer: Text 1 for Study and Comment* (Washington, D.C.: ICEL, 1984); an emended version, called *Prayer A,* was sent to the conferences for approval in 1986; see Page, 488.

Concern for language that excluded certain groups, especially women, from the prayers of the Church led ICEL to propose some modifications in the EPs in 1980.[22] Of these proposed revisions, the Holy See approved removal of the word "men" from the words of institution in 1981 for the United States, Canada, and New Zealand.[23] Two additional changes for Eucharistic Prayer IV were approved in 1985, which made the English translation conform to the 1975 Latin *editio typica altera*.[24]

These proposed changes were only intended to be a stopgap, since ICEL had announced that it was embarking on a comprehensive revision of the texts of the Sacramentary. The work began in 1982 with a workbook designed to elicit comment and suggestions for changes in the presidential prayers.[25] Three reports detailed the progress of revision. The first report (1988) included samples of the methods that ICEL was using for the revision: source criticism, literary criticism, philological study, and comparison with other translations into modern languages (such as French, German, and Italian).[26] The second report included more examples of revised translations, then added samples of original texts and gave some specimens of how it would present the texts in the revised Sacramentary.[27] The third report includes samples of the revision of the texts in the Order of Mass, including the prefaces and some of the EPs. Moreover, there are samples of the pastoral introductions, including the introduction to

22. *Eucharistic Prayers* (Washington, D.C.: ICEL, 1980). In addition to retouching the four Eucharistic Prayers from the Order of Mass and the three prayers for Masses with children and the two prayers for reconciliation, the Green Book included a Statement by the Advisory Committee of ICEL, signed by Archbishop Denis Hurley, "The Problem of Exclusive Language with Regard to Women," with an appended bibliography, on pp. 63–72.

23. The NCCB had approved all the changes in the 1980 Green Book in their meeting of November 1980; see *Bishops' Committee on the Liturgy Newsletter* 17 (January 1980); in *Bishops' Committee on the Liturgy Newsletter 1981–1985* (Washington, D.C.: NCCB, 1987) 1; hereafter cited as BCLN 81–85 and page number. The Holy See approved only the change eliminating the word "men" from the institution narrative; see *BCL Newsletter* 17 (1980); in BCLN 81–85, 45.

24. *BCL Newsletter* 21 (1985); in BCLN 81–85, 193–94.

25. *Consultation on Revision: The Roman Missal, Presidential Prayers* (Washington, D.C.: ICEL, 1982).

26. *Progress Report on the Revision of the Roman Missal* (Washington, D.C.: ICEL, 1988).

27. *Second Progress Report on the Revision of the Roman Missal* (Washington, D.C.: ICEL, 1990).

the EP.[28] The material from these progress reports was collated by ICEL and presented to the bishops in segments for approval. The first two segments and the pastoral introductions for the seasons were approved by the NCCB in November 1994; segment three, which included the EPs, was approved in June 1995; segment four and the pastoral introduction to the Order of Mass was approved in November 1995. Segments five and six were approved at the June 1996 meeting of the NCCB. Segments seven and eight were approved at the November 1996 meeting. After reconsidering some ICEL texts in June 1997, the BCL Secretariat assumed the task of the final editing of the Sacramentary with its adaptations for the United States—a task still proceeding at this writing.[29]

Clearly, ICEL's work on the revision of the texts of the Sacramentary, especially of the EPs, has not been done in a vacuum. In this next section, we will review the variety of work on the EP that has been done during the time of the ICEL revision process.

STUDIES ON THE EUCHARISTIC PRAYER SINCE 1980
Since the EP is one of the most studied aspects of the whole of the celebration of the Mass, we can only give a brief thematic overview of the variety and style of the work that has been done.[30]

HISTORY AND DEVELOPMENT OF THE EUCHARISTIC PRAYER
The original work of the Consilium was guided by the masters of the 1940s and 1950s such as Joseph Jungmann and Bernard Botte. In addition, Cipriano Vaggagini played a significant role in the development of the structure and even the content of the early prayers.[31]

28. *Third Progress Report on the Revision of the Roman Missal* (Washington, D.C.: ICEL, 1992).

29. The report of the various approvals can be found in *Bishops' Committee on the Liturgy Newsletter 1991–1995* (Chicago: Liturgy Training Publications, 1996) 191, 219–20, 233; *NCCB Committee on the Liturgy* 32 (1996) 25, 42; 33 (1997) 35, 46.

30. See the bibliography in *Liturgy Digest* 4 (2) (1997) 131–35 for works by North American authors writing in English.

31. Joseph A. Jungmann, *Missarum Sollemnia*, 2 vols. (Freiburg, 5th ed., 1962); ET, *The Mass of the Roman Rite*, 2 vols., trans. Francis Brunner (New York: Herder and Herder, 1951, 1955) from the 2nd German ed.; Bernard Botte, *La Tradition Apostolique de Saint Hippolyte: Essai de reconstitution*, LQF 39, 5th ed. (Münster: Aschendorff, 1989); Cipriano Vagaggini, *The Canon of the Mass and Liturgical Reform*, ed. P. Couglan (Staten Island: Alba House, 1967).

One of the issues that has captured the imagination of authors has been the origin of the EP. Did it originate in the four-part structure of the berakah as Audet proposed, or in the three-part meal prayers of the Passover Seder as Ligier studied, or a complex combination of the synagogue prayers and meal prayers as Bouyer describes?[32]

The discussion reached a new level of interest with the publication of a new work by the Italian Jesuit Cesare Giraudo, who proposed that the literary basis for the EP was the Jewish prayer form of the *todah*. This form is in two parts, a memorial in which God's powerful deeds are recalled and an invocation in which God is asked to continue acting in the same way. The two parts are connected by a transitional phrase linking the memorial and the invocation. Giraudo refers to the first part as anamnetic and the second as epicletic, and finds the theological center of the prayer in whichever part contains the "institutional narrative," a story which gives the warrant for the community's prayer. Hence a prayer is "anamnetic" or "epicletic" depending on where the institution narrative is found. Giraudo applies this methodology to biblical, synagogal, and Eucharistic Prayers.[33]

The response to Giraudo's work was mixed but also very productive. Thomas Talley introduced Giraudo's work to the English-speaking world and offered a critique that insists that the three-part forms of the meal prayers must also be considered when reflecting on the origins and structure of the prayer.[34] Enrico Mazza engaged the work

32. J. P. Audet, "Esquisse historique du genre littéraire de la 'bénédiction' et de l' 'eucharistie' chrétienne," *Revue biblique* 65 (1958) 371–99; L. Ligier, "De la Cène de Jésus à l'anaphore de l'Eglise," *La Maison Dieu* 97 (1966) 7–51; and "Les origines de la prière eucharistique," *Questions Liturgiques* 53 (1972) 181–202, among others; L. Bouyer, *Eucharist: Theology and Spirituality of the Eucharistic Prayer,* trans. C. Quinn (Notre Dame: University of Notre Dame Press, 1968). For a summary of the status of EP studies, see Benoit Thivierge, "The Eucharistic Prayer: From Jewish Prayer to Christian Anaphora," *Liturgical Ministry* 4 (Summer 1995) 97–108.

33. C. Giraudo, *La struttura letteraria de la preghiera eucaristica: Saggio sulla genesi letteraria di una forma: Toda veterotestamentaria, beraka giudaica, anafora cristiana,* Analecta Biblica 92 (Rome: Pontifical Biblical Institute, 1981); he continued this line of thought in *Eucaristia per la Chiesa: Prospettive teologiche sull'eucaristia a partire dalla "lex orandi,"* Aloisiana 22 (Rome: Gregorian University Press, 1989) and *Preghiere eucaristiche per la chiesa di oggi,* cited in n. 13 above.

34. "The Literary Structure of the Eucharistic Prayer," *Worship* 58 (1984) 404–20; revised version: "Sources and Structure of the Eucharistic Prayer," *Worship: Reforming Tradition* (Washington, D.C.: Pastoral Press, 1990) 11–34.

of Giraudo as well, and is better known in the English-speaking world because of his commentary on the Roman EPs.[35] His historical studies have consistently offered a position in contrast to Giraudo's, emphasizing the meal prayers as fundamentally threefold in their structure.[36] Richard McCarron offers an overview of recent historical study in his recent work *The Eucharistic Prayer at Sunday Mass.*[37] His purpose is to offer a perspective on the EP that will enable parish communities to pray the EP well each Sunday.

A work that demonstrates how reflection on the EP in North America has become an ecumenical enterprise is found in the work edited by Frank Senn, *New Eucharistic Prayers: An Ecumenical Study of Their Development and Structure.*[38] Prayers from the Roman, Episcopalian, Lutheran, Methodist, and Presbyterian traditions are studied historically, and then the various prayers are analyzed structurally, using a commonly agreed upon understanding of how an EP is put together. That consensus can be seen concretely in the Lima Liturgy prepared for the meeting of the Faith and Order Commission held there in 1982. Max Thurian of the Taizé Community was instrumental in this endeavor.[39]

General studies of the current Roman Catholic EPs can be found in the standard commentaries, such as those of Emminghaus, Cabié, Nocent, Moloney, and Meyer.[40]

Most recently he has written "Eucharistic Prayers, Past, Present and Future," *Revising the Eucharist: Groundwork for the Anglican Communion,* ed. David Holeton, Alcuin/GROW Liturgical Study 27 (Bramcote: Grove Books, 1994) 6–19.

35. *The Eucharistic Prayers of the Roman Rite,* trans. Matthew O'Connell (Collegeville: The Liturgical Press/Pueblo, 1986).

36. *The Origins of the Eucharistic Prayer,* trans. Ronald Lane (Collegeville: The Liturgical Press/Pueblo, 1995).

37. Chicago: Liturgy Training Publications, 1997.

38. New York: Paulist, 1987.

39. See *Baptism and Eucharist: Ecumenical Convergence in Celebration,* eds. Max Thurian and Geoffrey Wainwright (Grand Rapids, Mich.: Eerdmans, 1983); the Lima Liturgy is on pp. 241–55, including a commentary.

40. Johannes Emminghaus, *The Eucharist: Essence, Form, Celebration,* trans. Linda Maloney from the 1992 German ed. (Collegeville: The Liturgical Press, 1997); Robert Cabié, *The Eucharist,* The Church at Prayer II (Collegeville: The Liturgical Press, 1986); Adrien Nocent, "Storia della celebrazione dell'eucaristia," *Eucaristia: teologia e storia della celebrazione,* ed. S. Marsili and others, Anamnesis 3/2 (Casale Monferrato: Marietti, 1983) 187–270; Hans Bernhard Meyer, *Eucharistie: Geschichte, Theologie, Pastoral,* Gottesdienst der Kirche 4 (Regensburg: Pustet, 1989). See also the commentary by Raymond Moloney,

One last trend to mention in this section doubts our ability to get to any clear understanding of the origins of the EP. There is no archetypal original prayer, or even structure. There is an original multiplicity, each prayer of which must be studied on its own terms and in its own context, without generalizing to some original form or text. This skeptical approach has been advanced by Paul Bradshaw among others. He has done so in numerous articles, many of which have been revised and collected in his work *The Search for the Origins of Christian Worship*.[41]

STUDIES OF INDIVIDUAL EUCHARISTIC PRAYERS

Given this growing skepticism about the value of general studies of the EP, more and more energy has gone into the study of individual prayers. Curiously, though skepticism leads authors to study only a single prayer, being content to explore what this particular text says within its own literary-historical world, the comparative method is still one of the best ways to determine trends and meanings.[42] Clearly this implies relationship.

Studies of structural elements of the EP have become common. The study of prayers from various times and places implies underlying commonalities of composition and meaning. Most of these recent studies are of the new EPs, but are based on the scholarly consensus concerning the basic common structure, literary and theological, that underlies the EP. A recent ecumenical work includes the following structural elements: Preface; *Sanctus, Post-Sanctus*; the Institution Narrative; the *Anamnesis* / offering; the *Epiclesis*; the Intercessions /

Our Eucharistic Prayers in Worship, Preaching and Study, Theology and Life Series 14 (Wilmington, Del.: Michael Glazier, 1985).

41. *The Search for the Origins of Christian Worship: Sources and Methods for the Study of Early Liturgy* (New York: Oxford, 1992).

42. See the excellent bibliography in *Liturgy Digest* 4 (2) (1997) 131–35. For individual studies, see, for example, A. Gelston, *The Eucharistic Prayer of Addai and Mari* (Oxford: Clarendon, 1992); Maxwell Johnson, "A Fresh Look at the Prayers of Serapion of Thmuis," *Studia Liturgica* 22 (1992) 163–83; Walter Ray, "The Chiastic Structure of the Anaphora of Addai and Mari," *Studia Liturgica* 23 (1993) 187–93. For a comparative study, see John Fenwick, *The Anaphoras of St. Basil and St. James: An Investigation into Their Common Origin* (Rome: Pontifical Oriental Institute, 1992). See also Mazza's *The Origins of the Eucharistic Prayer* cited in n. 36 above; and *Essays on Early Eastern Eucharistic Prayers*, ed. Paul Bradshaw (Collegeville: The Liturgical Press/Pueblo, 1997). None of these studies lacks comparative elements.

commemorations; and the concluding Doxology.[43] Other works adopt a similar methodology.[44]

THE THEOLOGY OF THE CELEBRATION OF THE EUCHARIST AND THE EUCHARISTIC PRAYER

Today, theological treatment of the Eucharist must include a consideration of the EP as part of the data that must be considered in forming a synthesis. The role of the EP within the entire structure of the celebration is of primary importance. Without a clear understanding of the relationship between the Liturgy of the Word and the Liturgy of the Eucharist, the proper importance of the EP is not clearly understood. Second, the structure of the EP within itself and its theological content make a significant contribution to developing a comprehensive eucharistic theology.[45]

THE PASTORAL THEOLOGY OF THE EUCHARISTIC PRAYER

This historical, literary, and theological work has led to a particular approach in the pastoral celebration of the EP. One aspect is rooted in

43. *New Eucharistic Prayers,* 127–213, cited in n. 38 above.

44. See Brian Spinks, *The Sanctus in the Eucharistic Prayer* (Cambridge, Eng.: CUP, 1991); Marc Schneiders, "Acclamations in the Eucharistic Prayer," *Omnes Circumdastantes: Contributions Towards a History of the Role of the People in the Liturgy Presented to Herman Wegman,* ed. Charles Caspers and Marc Schneiders (Kampen, Netherlands: Kok, 1990) 78–100; Terrance Klein, "Institution Narratives at the Crossroads," *Worship* 67 (1993) 407–18; the bulk of the articles in *Gratias Agamus: Studien zum eucharistischen Hochgebet für Balthasar Fischer,* ed. Andreas Heinz and Heinrich Rennings (Freiburg: Herder, 1992).

45. For a recent analysis, see Michael G. Witczak, "The Manifold Presence of Christ in the Liturgy," *Theological Studies* 59 (December 1998) 680–702. Cesare Giraudo makes the case for this approach to eucharistic theology in *Eucaristia per la Chiesa* (n. 33 above) 1–14. In addition to the authors cited in Witczak's study (Edward Schillebeeckx, Joseph Powers, Alexander Gerken, David Power, Raymond Moloney, and Robert Sokolowski), see also Gordon Lathrop, *Holy Things: A Liturgical Theology* (Minneapolis: Fortress Augsburg, 1993); Edward Kilmartin, "The Catholic Tradition of Eucharistic Theology: Towards the Third Millennium," *Theological Studies* 55 (1994) 405–57; Chris Nwaka Egbulem, *The Power of Africentric Celebrations: Inspirations from the Zaire Liturgy* (New York: Crossroad, 1996); Brian Spinks, "Trinitarian Theology and the Eucharistic Prayer," *Studia Liturgica* 26 (1996) 209–24. Many of the articles in *Gratias Agamus* touch on the theology of the EP (see n. 44 above). See also the articles by Nathan Mitchell in *Liturgy Digest* 4 (2) (1997) and the volume by the faculty of the Catholic University of America, *Eucharist: Toward the Third Millennium* (Chicago: Liturgy Training Publications, 1997).

answering the question: "How is the Eucharistic Prayer the center and summit of the celebration?"[46] In order that the EP be experienced as the center and summit of the celebration of the Eucharist, a number of authors have reflected on how that prayer is prayed by both presider and assembly, both vocally and in gesture and posture.[47]

The original ICEL translations were affected by at least two factors: the scholarship about the EP that produced the Latin texts (and also the translation into English) and a particular theory about effective communication in English and hence translation into it.[48] The decision to revise the ICEL texts of the Sacramentary took place at a time

46. See GIRM 54; Andrew Ciferni and Elizabeth Hoffman, "The Eucharistic Prayer—Center and Summit?" *Liturgy 90* 23 (May–June 1992) 4–5, 15; Andrew Ciferni and J. Michael Thompson, "Repertoire and Ritual: The Communion Rite and the Eucharistic Prayer," *Pastoral Music* 17 (February–March 1993) 22–27; see also Richard McCarron, *The Eucharistic Prayer at Sunday Mass* (Chicago: Liturgy Training Publications, 1997) 50–75.

47. See Jan Michael Joncas, "*Hymnum Tuae Gloriae Canimus:* Toward an Analysis of the Vocal and Musical Expression of the Eucharistic Prayer in the Roman Rite," doctoral dissertation (Rome: Pontifical Liturgical Institute, 1991); John Leonard and Nathan Mitchell, *The Postures of the Assembly During the Eucharistic Prayer* (Chicago: Liturgy Training Publications, 1994); Charles Gardner, "Singing the Eucharistic Prayer: A Third Alternative," *Pastoral Music* 19 (December 1994–January 1995) 11–14; Donald Gray, "'Hands and Hocus-Pocus': The Manual Acts in the Eucharistic Prayer," *Worship* 69 (1995) 306–13; Zita Maier, "Standing at Eucharist: A Posture of Reverence," *National Bulletin on Liturgy* 28 (140) (1995) 37–50; John Baldovin, "*Accepit Panem:* The Gestures of the Priest at the Institution Narrative of the Eucharist," *Rule of Prayer, Rule of Faith: Essays in Honor of Aidan Kavanagh,* ed. Nathan Mitchell (Collegeville: The Liturgical Press/Pueblo, 1996) 123–39; Joseph Gelineau, "Making the Eucharistic Prayer an Act of the Whole Assembly," *Pastoral Music* 21 (February–March 1997) 26–32. See also Edward Foley and Mary McGann, *Music and the Eucharistic Prayer,* American Essays in Liturgy 8 (Collegeville: The Liturgical Press, 1988; originally Washington, D.C.: Pastoral Press); McCarron's book also has abundant reflection on the actual praying of the EP. The summer 1995 issue of *Liturgical Ministry* has articles that touch on the pastoral use of the EP, including Jeffrey Kemper and Steven Walter, "Need the Eucharistic Prayer Be Boring?" 120–26, and John McKenna, "Watch What You Pray: It Says What You Believe," 127–31. See the challenging article by Mark Searle, "Semiotic Analysis of Roman Eucharistic Prayer II," *Gratias Agamus* (n. 44 above) 469–87.

48. For the scholarship on the EP affecting the work of the Consilium, see n. 31 above. For the working principles for producing an English worship language, see the articles by Frederick McManus and John Page in *Shaping English Liturgy* cited in nn. 14 and 15 above.

when there had been advances in scholarship on the EP and changes in the idea of what is the proper kind of English to use for worship. The later ICEL texts are characterized by being "fuller and richer in vocabulary and syntax."[49] A more nuanced theology and a denser literary style are the result.

THE CHANGES INTRODUCED IN THE LATEST REVISION

Space does not permit a thorough analysis of all the changes proposed by ICEL in the translation of the EPs in the revised Sacramentary. We offer some examples which give a flavor of the work and show the dual concerns of theology and language.

EUCHARISTIC PRAYER I (THE ROMAN CANON)[50]

1967/68 text	1994 text	Latin text
In union with the whole Church	We pray in communion with the whole Church, with those whose memory we now honor: especially with Mary,	Communicantes, et memoriam venerantes,
we honor Mary, the ever-virgin mother of Jesus Christ our Lord and God.	the glorious and ever-virgin mother of Jesus Christ, our Lord and God.	in primis gloriosae semper Virginis Mariae, Genetricis Dei et Domini nostri Iesu Christi . . .

This revision highlights two issues: the desire to express the Latin in a richer way, and difficulties of capturing in English the very nuanced approach of the Latin rendering of Mary's relationship to Jesus Christ.[51]

49. See Page, 487.

50. 1967/68 text from *The Sacramentary* (New York: Catholic Book, 1974, 1985). 1994 text from *The Sacramentary, Segment Three: Order of Mass I* (Washington, D.C.: ICEL, 1994). Latin text from *Missale Romanum*, editio typica altera (Rome: Libreria Editrice Vaticana, 1975).

51. The notes in Segment Three (44–46) detail the doctrinal issues and various possible translations of the phrase.

1967/68 text	1994 text	Latin text
For ourselves, too, we ask some share in the fellowship of your apostles and martyrs, with John the Baptist, Stephen, Matthias, Barnabas, . . . , and all the saints. Though we are sinners, we trust in your mercy and love. Do not consider what we truly deserve, but grant us your forgiveness.	For ourselves, too, sinners who trust in your mercy and love, we ask some share in the fellowship of your apostles and martyrs, with John the Baptist, Stephen, Matthias, Barnabas, . . . , and all your saints. Welcome us into their company, not considering what we deserve, but freely granting us your pardon.	Nobis quoque peccatoribus famulis tuis, de multitudine miserationem tuarum sperantibus, partem aliquam et societatem donare digneris cum tuis sanctis Apostolis et Martyribus: cum Ioanne, Stephano, Matthia, Barnaba, . . . , et omnibus Sanctis tuis: intra quorum nos consortium, non aestimator meriti, sed veniae, quaesumus, largitor admitte.

Here again, the desire is to render the Latin more faithfully and to capture the theology more fully.

EUCHARISTIC PRAYER II

Two examples will capture the flavor the revisions.

1967/68 text	1994 text	Latin text
For our sake he opened his arms on the cross; he put an end to death and revealed the resurrection. In this he fulfilled your will and won for you a holy people.	To accomplish your will and to gain for you a holy people, he stretched out his arms on the cross, that he might break the chains of death and make known the resurrection.	Qui voluntatem tuam adimplens et populum tibi sanctum acquirens extendit manus cum pateretur, ut mortem solveret et resurrectionem manifestaret.

The order of the English follows the Latin more closely, but more importantly, the concreteness of the Latin comes through more clearly.

1967/68 text	1994 text	Latin text
Lord, remember your Church throughout the world;	Lord, remember your Church throughout the world;	Recordare, Domine, Ecclesiae tuae toto orbe diffusae,
make us grow in love, together with N. our Pope,	make us perfect in love together with N. our Pope, N. our Bishop,	ut eam in caritate perficias una cum Papa nostro N. et Episcopo
N. our bishop, and all the clergy.	and all who minister to your people.	nostro N. et universo clero.

ICEL argues in the notes that "clergy" with its current canonical overtones does not capture the ambiguity of the Latin *"clerus."*[52]

EUCHARISTIC PRAYER III

Here we look at the first epiclesis for an example of how ICEL is translating the nuances of the Latin more completely.

1967/68 text	1994 text	Latin text
And so, Father, we bring you these gifts.	And so, Lord God, we humbly pray:	Supplices ergo te, Domine, deprecamur,
We ask you to make them holy by the power of your Spirit,	by the power of your Spirit sanctify these gifts	ut haec munera, quae tibi sacranda detulimus,
that they may become the body ✠ and blood	we have brought before you,	eodem Spiritu sanctificare digneris,
of your Son, our Lord Jesus Christ,	that they may become the body ✠ and blood	ut Corpus et ✠ Sanguis fiant
at whose command we celebrate this Eucharist.	of your Son, our Lord Jesus Christ,	Filii tui Domini nostri Iesu Christi,
	at whose command we celebrate this Eucharist.	cuius mandato haec mysteria celebramus.

The order is more faithful to the Latin and captures the directness of the epicletic prayer.

EUCHARISTIC PRAYER IV

One example from this revision will demonstrate the attention ICEL paid to recent research on the EP.

52. Segment Three, 55–56.

1967/68 text	1994 text	Latin text
. . . and looking forward to his coming in glory, we offer you his body and blood, the acceptable sacrifice which brings salvation to the whole world.	. . . and, looking forward to his coming in glory, we offer you the sacrifice of his body and blood, an offering acceptable to you, which brings salvation to all the world.	. . . et exspectantes ipsius adventum in gloria, offerimus tibi eius Corpus et Sanguinem, sacrificium tibi acceptabile et toti mundo salutare.

The text of EP IV has been criticized for its too direct language of "offering the Body and Blood of Christ." See, for instance, Mazza's comment: "What is offered is the sacrament, not the historical events of the passion and resurrection, in which Christ was victim, sacrifice, altar, and priest: He was his own priest and offered once and for all."[53]

THE PASTORAL INTRODUCTION

The Pastoral Introduction to the EP summarizes material from the GIRM and other sources. The first part offers a theological understanding of the role of the EP in the whole celebration. It echoes GIRM 54, calling the prayer "the center and summit of the entire celebration," but then continues by describing how it "sums up what it means for the Church to celebrate the eucharist."[54]

The Pastoral Introduction then details the structure of the EP. It is instructive to compare it with the list found in GIRM 55:

GIRM 55	1994 text[55]
	Dialogue
Thanksgiving (primarily the preface)	Preface
Acclamation (Sanctus)	Sanctus/acclamation
Epiclesis	Epiclesis
Institution narrative and consecration	Institution narrative and consecration
	Memorial acclamation
Anamnesis	Anamnesis and Offering
Offering	Intercessions
Intercessions	Doxology
Final doxology	

53. Mazza, *The Eucharistic Prayers of the Roman Rite*, 178–79.
54. Segment Three, 169.
55. Segment Three, 170–76.

The Pastoral Introduction makes a couple of changes, which highlight the theological and pastoral concerns of the document. First of all, it begins with the dialogue between priest and people. Here we find reflected the fundamentally dialogical character of the prayer. In speaking of the Preface, the Introduction focuses on the way that the Preface constitutes the beginning of the prayer rather than being simply preparatory. The Introduction adds a section on the memorial acclamation and explains it as a confession of faith by the people. The document combines its treatment of the anamnesis and the offering, since the two concepts are integrally bound in all the prayers.

The Pastoral Introduction then uses the theology of each particular section to comment about how the celebration of the prayer should reinforce its meaning: song, gesture, and posture all combine to draw the attention of people and priest to the importance of what they are doing. There should be a congruity between importance, word, and action.

ISSUES THAT NEED TO BE ADDRESSED
AND HOW THE ICEL REVISIONS AFFECT THEM
As we saw in our survey of recent literature about the EP, there is much concern about how this "center and summit" of our celebration should stand out clearly as such and not simply languish as a long boring interlude between the homily and receiving Communion.

ICEL has addressed concerns about fidelity to the Latin text and to the richness of the theological tradition by revising its early work in the light of both classical and more recent scholarship, and good English style. Clearly, since there is little agreement even in literary circles about what constitutes good English style, ICEL's work will still need to bear the brunt of criticism.

Concerns about participation by the whole community have been addressed in several ways. First of all, the revised translation with a richer language will, it is hoped, engage the imagination of the assembly in a more profound way. Emphasis on the dialogical character of the prayer will serve both in catechesis and celebration as a catalyst for both priest and assembly to take appropriate responsibility for the prayer. Especially the role of singing, even of the whole prayer, is highlighted and needs further attention from composers, musicians, priests, and assembly alike. Gestures that visibly articulate in a nonverbal way the meaning of the words will go far in allowing the prayer to speak.

ICEL addresses concerns about the structure of the prayer in two ways. First of all, a clear structural analysis of the prayer articulates both the theological and pastoral issues it wishes to develop. At the same time, the document insists on the unity of the prayer and stresses the importance of voice and gesture underlining its fundamental oneness.

Anscar Chupungco has offered us a vision of an inculturated liturgy that respects both the long, rich tradition of the Roman Rite and at the same time allows the truths of God's action in the world through Jesus Christ in the power of the Holy Spirit to be expressed in ways that have meaning for the people of a given place and time. The ICEL project of revising the Eucharistic Prayers is one important step in that journey.

Gordon W. Lathrop

The Revised Sacramentary in EcumenicalAffirmation and Admonition[1]

In 1998 four Reformed and Lutheran churches in North America entered into an epoch-making *Formula of Agreement* which restored full communion between these long-divided communities. In the agreement, the parties covenanted together to continue to engage in an ongoing theological and pastoral conversation, especially focused around areas of historic disagreement but also turned to current issues of mission and practice. They called that conversation "mutual affirmation and admonition."[2]

Such a characterization of the conversation which might go on between church bodies has enormous ecclesial significance, and that not only for American "denominations." Imagine that local churches, the very eucharistic assemblies the revised Sacramentary and other recent liturgical books intend to serve, would understand themselves as called to "mutual affirmation and admonition" with other local churches, those nearby and those far away. Imagine that such a mature dialogue would mark the very "communion of churches" which makes up the unity of the Church, say the communion between the

1. This article is intended as an homage of thanksgiving for Anscar Chupungco, O.S.B., who, in his work with both the World Council of Churches and the Lutheran World Federation, has provided a remarkable example of ecumenical affirmation and admonition, graciously, courteously but profoundly applied to liturgical celebration, and who, in his person, has provided us all with an embodied sign of prayer for Christian unity.

2. See Keith F. Nickle and Timothy F. Lull, eds., *A Common Calling: The Witness of Our Reformation Churches in North America Today* (Minneapolis: Augsburg/Fortress, 1993).

Church in Chicago or the Church in Manila and the Church in Rome itself. Even more, imagine that local assemblies and communions of such assemblies would engage in this conversation with other such assemblies and communions with whom they find themselves united in the one baptism and the one gospel but still visibly and tragically divided in mission and at the Eucharist. Mutual affirmation and admonition can be one means toward communion between divided churches and one means for the expression of mature common life between local churches already in communion.

The idea of such a conversation can be specifically applied to the liturgy of the churches as well.[3] Indeed, books like the revised Sacramentary might be best understood as concrete forms of such "mutual affirmation and admonition," ways in which a local assembly might have its practice both encouraged and helpfully criticized. After all, the Eucharist exists in the local church before a revised liturgical book reaches that assembly. But, in this case, the new liturgical book would come to that assembly representing the combined wisdom of persons who have arisen in a whole range of other local churches— scholars and teaching bishops, priests, and praying poets—who pass on the *ordo* of the Eucharist in new clarity, accompanied with new insight into its tradition, new translations, and adaptations of its *editio typica* texts, and new proposals for the lively combination of the ancient "genius of the Roman liturgy" with the genius of the contemporary English-speaking cultures. The book itself, then, understood in such a way, would represent and enable not so much the legal enforcement of a new text as a challenging, deepening conversation between one local assembly, the assembly that takes up the book with seriousness, and that communion of many assemblies which is brought to expression in the book. Of course, the conversation can flow back the other way, as the many passages concerning local adaptation and local planning found throughout the revised Sacramentary make clear. In any case, a new Sacramentary will not bring the liturgy to a local assembly. But it will bring a new and renewing conversation between that assembly and the universal Church as that church is represented, in this case, by a communion of English-speaking churches acting through their bishops, teachers, and litur-

3. For one example, see my article, "The Worship Books in Mutual Affirmation and Admonition: Liturgy as a Source for Lutheran-Reformed Unity," *Reformed Liturgy and Worship* 21 (2) (1997) 88–92.

gists. Furthermore, such a responsible revision also represents a conversation of affirmation and admonition, in a secondary sense, with other linguistic communities within the Roman Catholic Church who are also seeking to express the authentic tradition in the authentic cultural conditions of their own present situations.

But can this liturgy book, intended for the use of local assemblies who are bound to communion with the Roman Catholic Church, also play a role in a mutual conversation with other assemblies and communions as well? Can other churches hear the book as also addressed, in some secondary or tertiary—but still *important*—way, to them? And may they also respond, in affirmation and admonition? If we belong to each other in Christ, in spite of our divisions, can we also say of this Sacramentary what Tertullian says: "Whatever belongs to those who are of us belongs to us"?[4]

Indeed, something like this idea of ecumenical affirmation and admonition has already been applied to liturgy by the 1994 Faith and Order consultation on *koinonia* in worship:

"[T]he patterns of word and table, of catechetical formation and baptism, of Sunday and the week, of *Pascha* and the year, and of assembly and ministry around these things—the principal pairs of the Christian liturgy—do give us a basis for a mutually encouraging conversation between the churches. Churches may rightly ask each other about the local inculturation of this *ordo*. They may call each other towards a maturation in the use of this pattern or a renewed clarification of its central characteristics or, even, towards a conversion to its use. . . . This same pattern or *ordo* of Christian worship is a major basis for the koinonia between local churches, a koinonia spanning both space and time, uniting churches of the New Testament times, of the sweep of Christian history and of the present oikoumene. Such a koinonia can only be enriched by those authentic forms of inculturation which the *ordo* may have taken in each local church, not diminished."[5]

Let it be said clearly: this revised Sacramentary is such an authentic form of the inculturation of the *ordo* of Christian worship in the cultures of the current English-speaking world. Or, rather, since it is

4. *De virginibus velandis* 2.2: *nostrum est quodcunque nostrorum est.*
5. Report of the Ditchingham Consultation, 7 and 8b, in Thomas F. Best and Dagmar Heller, eds., *So We Believe, So We Pray: Towards Koinonia in Worship*, Faith and Order Paper No. 171 (Geneva: World Council of Churches, 1995) 7–8.

only a *book,* not the event of the liturgy itself, this Sacramentary must rightly be called a remarkable fruit, sign, and encouragement of such authentic inculturation. This book, published and freely circulating, would be an enrichment of our *koinonia.* Then let the conversation which belongs to *koinonia* between the churches take up this book. Let the churches which have no formal relationship to the book nonetheless consider it, seeing what encouragement and critique it may offer to their practice. And then, gently and with humility, let the conversation flow back toward the book and the communion of churches it represents, in affirmation and admonition. May such a reception and conversation soon be possible. And, in the future, may *all* of our liturgical books come to be received in such a wider circle of affirmation and admonition.

Indeed, the first affirmation about this book which a person who does not belong to the Roman communion must speak is the urgent prayer that its excellence may soon be released to local assembly use and thereby be made available to the ecumenical conversation.

LISTENING TO THE SACRAMENTARY IN THE
OTHER CHURCHES

But a down payment may be made on that conversation. The churches which are not in communion with Rome need to listen to what is being proposed in this book. And they need to begin to respond. It is not just that whatever happens with the Roman liturgy is important to those of us who also share in the inheritance of the Western rite and in the work of that rite's continual cultural contextualization. It is also and specifically that this particular book is marked by such excellence of insight and such authenticity in inculturation that persons who care about worship in all the churches need its witness. Not so that they may use it directly, but so that its clarity and its spirit might also challenge and support their own liturgical life.

In what ways? Even now, we can make some estimate of matters of importance which would be addressed to us indirectly were we listen to this Roman book. Here is one short list:

The Sacramentary can be read as affirming in other, non-Roman liturgical communities

—the movement toward a full and clear use of *word and table*—full reading of three passages of Scripture, strong psalmody as response to the first reading, strong biblical preaching, and the full *eucharistia* and Communion—as the central Sunday event in all communities;

—the growing awareness that *assembly* around these central matters is the primary form of church;

—the development of many different *ministries* in the Sunday liturgy as expressive of that meaning of assembly;

—the widespread use of *common English translations,* the fruit of the work of the ecumenical English Language Liturgical Consultation, for core liturgical texts;

—the movement toward the *general intercessions* or prayers of the faithful becoming real prayers of the assembly, crafted in each local place and prayed for real needs of church and world "beyond the concerns of the local assembly" itself (Introduction to the Order of Mass, 97);

—the development of a variety of interchangeable *introductory rites,* all sharing the intention of reconstituting "church" as the assembly of the baptized, reconciled in Christ and gathered in the presence of the triune God around the gift of word and sacrament;

—and, even, the growing and shared wisdom which places brief pastoral *announcements* needed for the current celebration in the course of the gathering rites and brief congregational announcements related to mission and service in the concluding rite.

These matters are not Roman Catholic peculiarities. Neither were they invented by Protestants. They are, rather, shared matters of liturgical wisdom—our common inheritance—expressed in current English-speaking cultural contexts. They all can be enacted without any loss of treasured particularity within a diversity of ritual practice. But the renewed strength of their presence in the revised Sacramentary can be received by other liturgical communities in the process of renewal as a voice of affirmation and a sign of convergence.

Still more, the revised Sacramentary can also be read as challenging other liturgical communities to continue to work for parish liturgical renewal especially by accentuating two things:

—the development of a beautiful *contemporary English style of prayer* which makes fine use of biblical images and of richly inclusive language while also attending to the suitability of the language for oral, communal proclamation;

—and the availability of fine *pastoral introductions* to the materials, flow, and meaning of the liturgy.

Indeed, it is these two matters which anyone picking up the two volumes of this book will first note: the Sacramentary is rich with clear and beautiful texts for prayer, and it is provided with profoundly conceived and remarkably helpful introductions to the liturgy and its occasions. The sooner the texts of this book—especially the Introduction to the Order of Mass, the alternate, Scripture-based Opening Prayers, and both the translations and the new adaptation of the *Exsultet* of the Easter Vigil—are published, the better our mutual conversation about renewal will be served.

Again, it is not that either the Scripture-based Opening Prayers, for example, nor the Introduction to the Order of Mass ought to be used directly in other communities. One might quibble a little over whether the texts of the Opening Prayers are not sometimes a little too long. And the conception of priesthood present in the Introduction remains, in places, problematic for many communities of the Reformation. But the point is not that this is a book which could be used in other than Roman Catholic assemblies. Rather the spirit of this book—and some of its details—should rightly urge other liturgical assemblies and communions to take up again, with refreshed interest, the ongoing tasks of *words for worship*, both in prayer-texts and in catechesis. Recent publications in the Reformation churches—take for example, the Presbyterian *Book of Common Worship*—have similarly been marked by the great interest in finding a beautiful, biblical, and inclusive language which continues to express trinitarian orthodoxy. That same Presbyterian book, itself a book which is rightly and widely considered to represent a harvest of several decades of ecumenical liturgical work, also includes a remarkable pastoral introduction to the shape and flow of the "Service for the Lord's Day," the communal liturgy of word and table.[6] But the language task—given the challenges of linguistic change, the insights of feminism, the new awareness of the necessity of using biblical images, and the burgeoning reflection on the Trinity which marks today's finest Christian theology—is probably a hundred-year undertaking that will continue to require our best attention. Furthermore, we all share the challenge to put the flow and meaning of the liturgy into words that will teach

6. *Book of Common Worship* (Louisville, Ky.: Westminster/John Knox, 1993) 33–45.

the participant assembly, enable good liturgical planning, and evoke fine leadership from the ministers of the assembly, and this challenge is never-ending. The revised Sacramentary is remarkable encouragement to liturgists of all communities to continue the work.

RESPONDING IN AFFIRMATION: *ORDO MISSAE*

A list can also begin to be made of ways in which other churches might respond this book and to the English-language Roman Catholic communities behind it. The list of affirmations would be long. It would included all of the matters listed above: word and sacrament in balance; liturgical assembly as church; many ministries; the use of the ecumenical ELLC texts when they are available; strong help for the local crafting and leading of the intercessions; beautiful introductory rites; an appropriate liturgical and ecclesial role for announcements; biblical imagery and inclusive language in the translation and adaptation of texts; and the expansion of rubrics and general instructions into clear and profound pastoral introductions. But more matters could be listed: the remarkable rubrics and pastoral explanations for both the procession with the gifts and the Communion procession, for example, or the extensive use of music throughout the rite, so that the entire event of Mass is conceived as musical.

But the most significant nomination for ecumenical affirmation in the book may seem at first a simple matter of typographic arrangement, of "presentation of the text," and not a matter of substance at all. It is the strong presence of "a schematic structural outline," an *ordo missae*, as the organizational principal of the entire Sacramentary and of its major celebrations, "showing at a glance the sequence and articulation of their component parts."[7] The importance of this *ordo* is far greater than one might at first presume. Of course, the outline provides a key to the materials of the book, so that planners and leaders may be able to readily find their way through this book of options. Furthermore, this *ordo* gives primary shape to the pastoral Introduction, so that parish catechesis can be easily structured around the shape of the celebration. An *ordo*-based approach to the liturgy does indeed give strength and facility to planning, leadership, and catechesis, giving teachers a pattern for their teaching and giving leaders assistance with focus, accent, and understanding as they move through the flow of the liturgy.

7. Foreword, I:17.

But this use of the *ordo* does much more. By the presence of the great outline of the event at key places in the book, the Sacramentary itself is seen to support the idea that the liturgy is not primarily *text*, but *event*. The book provides texts for this event, but the event itself is larger than any texts can contain. Indeed, what links the churches together, in the communion of churches, is not primarily an authoritative *editio typica* of texts, but the widespread shape of a communal event around the crucified and risen Jesus Christ, present in word and sacrament. The texts of the Roman typical edition—and the local contextualizations of these texts—all must serve the presence of that event in local assemblies. So, it is first of all that *ordo*, that shaped and meaningful event, which gives the churches the concrete basis for a local adaptation and inculturation which remains in communion with the other churches.[8] And it is that *ordo* itself which gives a basic ground for recognition, let alone mutual affirmation and recognition, between the churches.

Indeed, the *ordo* of the Sacramentary, when it is finally published, should be seen side-by-side with the shape of the liturgy as it has been set out recently in a great variety of other liturgical books and liturgical theologies. These include the already mentioned Presbyterian *Book of Common Worship*,[9] but also Orthodox,[10] Anglican,[11] North American Lutheran,[12] German Reformed, Evangelical, and United Church[13] sources. These comparisons will demonstrate the astonishing ecumenical convergence in the churches, especially in regard to their fundamental eucharistic celebrations. Such convergence lies behind the ecumenical *ordo* to which the Faith and Order consultation

8. See Anscar J. Chupungco, "Two Methods of Liturgical Inculturation," S. Anita Stauffer, ed., *Christian Worship: Unity in Cultural Diversity* (Geneva: Lutheran World Federation, 1996) 81; and "Liturgical Inculturation and the Search for Unity," *So We Believe, So We Pray*, 61.

9. "Basic Movement of the Service for the Lord's Day" and "An Outline of the Service for the Lord's Day," *Book of Common Worship*, 33, 46.

10. Most importantly, Alexander Schmemann, *Introduction to Liturgical Theology* (New York: St. Vladimir's Seminary Press, 1975) 32–36.

11. *Book of Common Prayer* (New York: Church Hymnal Corporation, 1979) 400–01; and *A New Zealand Prayerbook* (Auckland: Collins, 1989) 511. Cf. Paul Gibson, *Patterns of Celebration: Layers of Meaning in the Structure of the Eucharist* (Toronto: Anglican Book Centre, 1998).

12. "Holy Communion: Shape of the Rite," *With One Voice: A Lutheran Resource for Worship* (Minneapolis: Augsburg/Fortress, 1995) 8–9.

13. *Erneuerte Agende* (Hannover, 1990) 32 and 42.

at Ditchingham referred.[14] And this convergence also comes to strong expression in the proposal now being circulated as a way to continue the momentum of the so-called "Lima Liturgy" and as a way, therefore, to celebrate the Eucharist in ecumenical contexts. This proposal is itself *ordo*-based.[15] The revised Sacramentary joins this ecumenical ferment, itself the result of the astonishingly ecumenical liturgical thought of the twentieth century.

But the *ordo missae* of the Sacramentary, presented in its fine schematic structural outlines, ought to be strongly affirmed not only because of its catechetical and ecumenical value. The *ordo* is also a tool of the profound Christian meaning desperately needed in our present cultural situations. While the Roman Catholic communities for which the Sacramentary is primarily intended may not be authorized to adopt any of the other competing patterns currently circulating in the marketplace of religions, they do often experience the temptation to obscure the *ordo missae* with secondary matters. On the other hand, North American Protestant churches—and churches of the world which are influenced by their choices—have been drawn toward patterns of worship which accentuate those words and music which move the individual Self toward conversion or, to use more modern language, engage in the "marketing" of personal "happiness" and the "meeting of needs." Such religion, for all of its Christian vocabulary, is easily tempted to Gnosticism.[16] The same interest in "meeting needs" and satisfying the religious longings of the Self, however, may be operative also in the very worship patterns which a local Roman Catholic assembly may allow to obscure the central movement of the Liturgy of Eucharist.

On the contrary, the flow of meaning found in the ecumenical *ordo missae*, for which the revised Sacramentary may stand as such a sterling exemplar, proposes entirely different religious values. An assembly

14. See above.

15. See Thomas F. Best and Dagmar Heller, eds., *Eucharistic Worship in Ecumenical Contexts: The Lima Liturgy and Beyond* (Geneva: World Council of Churches, 1998) 29–35.

16. The trenchant, if somewhat overstated, study of this phenomenon is Harold Bloom's *The American Religion* (New York: Simon and Schuster, 1992). For a comparison of the patterns of worship in such market-driven communities with the classic, ecumenical *ordo,* see my "New Pentecost or Joseph's Britches? Reflections on the History and Meaning of the Worship *ordo* in the Megachurches," *Worship* 72 (6) (November 1998).

gathers, as church is reconstituted. This assembly is not just a collection of individuals on a religious quest for personal fulfillment, but the eschatological *ecclesia Dei*. Then the word of God is read and preached and sung in that assembly. The *ordo* bears witness that the triune God has been active in this actual, material world, with its actual history, and that this action now comes to us. The eucharistic meal then gathers this present assembly into participation in the incarnation, death, risen presence, and future of this God, and the concluding rites quickly send that same assembly into the paths of the resultant mission and service. The accents on community, history, eschatology, materiality, Trinity, incarnation, mission, and service are, of course, radically different than the themes of Gnosticism and the religion of Self-realization. These accents belong to the *ordo missae*. One might say that this classic, ecumenical *ordo* reenacts the structure of the orthodox gospel books: the biblical stories and gospel pericopes lead the community to the meal, to the participation in the death and resurrection of Christ, and so into renewed care for this real earth; the proclamation of the past leads the present assembly into the future. This *ordo* itself—and not some misguided accent on "correct" texts— is the primary mark of orthodox, faithful Christianity. As the revised Sacramentary is published, the churches will need to affirm its *ordo*-based presentation.

RESPONDING IN ADMONITION: PRAYERS OVER THE GIFTS
But the churches will also need to respond with some modest words of admonition. While the list of matters for such a critical conversation will be quite short, ecumenical honesty will require that a few be discussed. It might include these:

—the idea that communal hymnody ought to be considered as a serious part of the *ordo* itself, not simply an occasional, thematic decoration for the movement of the ministers;

—the question as to whether the penitential rite really ought to be combined with the *kyrie*, even if there are many other options for introductory rites;

—the urging that the *verba institutionis* of the Eucharist, the words of Christ concerning bread and cup, be proclaimed, in English at least, in a strong present tense ("which is given" not "which will be given up"), building on the Greek and biblical tradition and making clear the presence of Christ in the current event, not our imaginative reconstruction of the past Supper;[17]

—and the plea that the pastoral Introduction itself (and all of our future pastoral introductions, in all the churches) acknowledge the ecumenical significance of the *ordo,* thereby assisting the ecumenical theme to enter into local liturgical catechesis.

While the discussion of these matters might be lively, the most serious ecumenical discussion might be held around the question of the current liturgical role of the prayer over the gifts. Of course, at this classical *locus* we enter into the ancient and still unresolved debate over the "sacrifice of the Mass" and its verbal expression. But the point here is not to ask Roman Catholics to become Protestants. Nor is it to ignore the wonderful work that the revised Sacramentary has done on this very liturgical issue, in harmony with many Roman Catholic theologians who continue to think about the nature of "sacrifice."

In the book, the prayers over the gifts are radically simplified, especially when the assembly sings while the gifts are being brought to the altar. In such a circumstance, strongly encouraged by the Sacramentary, the *berakoth* formulae ("Blessed are you . . .") are said silently by the presider, and the only audible prayers before the Eucharistic Prayer are the proper prayer over the gifts and an unchanged translation of the old *orate fratres* exchange. These proposals mark some considerable progress in clarity and simplification.

Even more, the Introduction to the Order of Mass speaks remarkably about the reasons for this simplifications and about the rationale for the presentation of the gifts at all:

"(100) At the beginning of the liturgy of the eucharist the gifts that will become the Lord's body and blood are brought to the altar. This taking of bread and wine is a preparation of the gifts. It is not in itself the sacrifice or offering, but a preparation for the eucharistic prayer, the great act of blessing and thanksgiving which constitutes the Church's memorial offering of Christ's sacrifice, and for communion. (101) The Church encourages the faithful to bring forward, and even to provide, the elements through which Christ's offering will be made present, together with money and other gifts for the sustenance of Christ's body, especially the poor and the needy. . . . (105) The

17. See Frank C. Senn, ed., *New Eucharistic Prayers: An Ecumenical Study of Their Development and Structure* (New York: Paulist Press, 1987) 144.

procession with the gifts is a powerful expression of the assembly's participation in the eucharist and in the social mission of the Church. It is an expression of the humble and contrite heart, the dispossession of self that is a necessary prerequisite for making the true offering which the Lord Jesus gave his people to make with him. The procession with the gifts expresses also our eager willingness to enter into the 'holy exchange' with God: 'accept the offerings you have given us, that we in turn may receive the gift of yourself.'"

These are wonderful texts. But the problem is that this purpose of the preparation and procession does not come clearly to expression in most of the presidential prayers over the gifts that follow. Certainly not in the *orate fratres* dialogue, where the priest is the lone sacrificer, and where the christological transformation of "sacrifice" is entirely absent. But also not in the proper texts. There the theme of the "holy exchange," looking forward to the action of *eucharistia* and Communion, is indeed quite beautifully present and quite frequent:

"Lord . . . let this present expression of our reverence become for us the pledge of eternal redemption" (Advent 1).

or:

"Fill your Church with the power of your Spirit, O God, that our thanksgiving over this bread and wine may become our communion in your love" (Maundy Thursday Chrism Mass).

But, in spite of the Introduction's clarity, the theme of humility, what Max Thurian called "the crisis at the offertory,"[18] our inability to bring anything except our need of God, is much more rarely present in the actual texts. And the theme of social mission and concern for the poor, a natural companion to this humility in Christian thought, is hardly present at all.

Again, though a Christian from Reformation heritage might raise this question with the communion of churches represented in this book, the point is not to ask Roman Catholics to become Protestant. It is rather to urge that the meaning of the procession with the gifts, so magisterially taught in the Introduction, in profound accord with the "genius of the Roman rite," might come to expression in the "sta-

18. Max Thurian, *The Eucharistic Memorial* 2 (Richmond, Va.: John Knox, 1961) 107.

tional" prayer of that procession. Without profound humility and a sense of solidarity with the hungry, our described religious "exchanges" can too easily become *do ut des*, "I give to you, God, so that you might be obligated to give to me."

But here is a further question: Why pray an audible prayer at all? In spite of the long Western tradition, is an offertory prayer really needed? Is not the Eucharistic Prayer itself the great prayer that is appropriate to this moment? Is any other needed in the flow of the *ordo*? And should not the Eucharistic Prayer be clear about our humility, our need, our solidarity with the hungry and the dying, and God's gracious gift of the happy exchange, the *admirabile commercium*, in Christ?[19] I hope the churches which may come to use and treasure this revised Sacramentary might also treasure such questions, no matter how they answer them.

The book itself, after all, has arisen out of a history of liturgical affirmation and admonition. Given the chance to see the communal light of day, this book is destined to continue that tradition in the conversation of the churches. Here is a magnificent book, challenging and encouraging us all.

19. On these and related questions, see my article "The Bodies on Nevado Ampato: A Further Note on Offering and Offertory," *Worship* 71 (6) (November 1997) 546–54.

Bernardo Ma. Pérez, O.S.B.

Anscar—Monk Extraordinary

José Herminio Javier Chupungco was sixteen years old when he was admitted as a postulant to the Abbey of Our Lady of Montserrat in Manila on May 30, 1956. The following year, having finished high school at San Beda College, which is administered by the Benedictine monks, he was received into the novitiate by Abbot Pedro Celestino Gusi and was given the name Anscario, not after St. Anscar, the Benedictine bishop and missionary, but after a monk of the Abbey of Montserrat in Barcelona, Spain, a good friend of Abbot Gusi, who was killed during the Spanish civil war.

Anscar is the youngest of seven children—five sons and two daughters—of Estanislao Chupungco and Dominga Javier of Cainta, a prosperous small town in Rizal province, not far from Manila. The Chupungco residence is on the town's main street, next to the municipal hall, where the trial of Christ is staged on Good Friday. Across is the parish church, a massive stone building dating back to the Spanish colonial period.

Estanislao was originally from Pasig, a nearby town, but when he married Dominga, he moved to her hometown. He was a school teacher who worked hard and lived frugally, saving as much as he could for the education of his children. His grandfather, probably named Chu Pung Co, came to the Philippines from Fookien, China, in the nineteenth century. He settled in Pasig, engaged in trade, and quickly acquired a fortune and extensive property. Estanislao recalled that as a child he was carried around in a sedan chair. Estanislao's father died when he was still a child, so an uncle, his father's brother, became the administrator of the estate. Unfortunately, the uncle gambled and lost the children's inheritance.

When he was old enough, Estanislao was employed as a school teacher. His hard work was complemented by Dominga's business sense. They sent all their children through school and enabled them to have a college education. Their eldest son, Bienvenido, became an accountant and rose to the position of executive vice president of the Pepsi-Cola Bottling Corporation. The second son, Cesar, is a physician. The eldest daughter, Fe, is a pharmacist, and a son, Godofredo, and a daughter, Aurora, became dentists. Estanislao, the fourth son, is a chemical engineer who became an executive of a large mining company. Being engaged in the teaching profession, Anscar is the only one who followed in his father's footsteps.

Like his brothers and sisters, Anscar had his early education at the Cainta Elementary School. Then he enrolled at the high school of the University of Santo Tomas, the Dominican university in Manila. Desiring to become a priest, he transferred to Our Lady of Guadalupe Minor Seminary. There he heard about the Benedictine abbey in Manila, and applied for admission. He pronounced his simple vows in 1958, and three years later, his solemn vows. The abbey had its own school of philosophy and theology, but Anscar and a few other monks were sent to the University of Santo Tomas. He obtained his licentiate in philosophy, *magna cum laude,* in 1961 and his licentiate in theology, *magna cum laude,* in 1965. He studied philosophy in the years before Vatican II, but his theological formation was influenced by the spirit of the council. While a theology student, Anscar taught at the abbey—fourth-year Latin—Virgil's *Aeneid*—to the postulants, and Hebrew to the theology students.

In the early 1960s, the abbey's theology students ran a mimeographed in-house periodical, *The Cloister,* that contained articles on theology, spirituality, monasticism, philosophy, psychology, literature, and art, as well as poetry, reports on abbey activities, and a humor section. One issue had a symposium on racial discrimination.

A front-page story in a 1962 issue, headlined "Fr. Prior Sparks Liturgy Movement," reported that Fr. Bernardo Lopez sent two monks to Rome for liturgical studies as "the first concrete step in his plan to establish a Liturgical Center in the Abbey." One monk was assigned to take monastic studies, and the other, sacred art. In the same issue Anscar had an essay, "How to Become an Atheist," a critique of Nietzsche.

In the April 1963 issue, Anscar had two essays, "Meditation on Metaphysics" and "Meditation on Becoming." Shifting to theology in later issues, Anscar established his reputation for advanced thinking in "The Virginal Motherhood of the Church" and "Apostolic Preaching and the Sources of Revelation." He discussed the role of the laity in the Church in "Among the People of God" in the Easter 1964 issue. It is interesting to note that the Dogmatic Constitution on the Church, which has a chapter on the laity, was promulgated on November 21, 1964, and the Decree on the Apostolate of the Laity, on November 18, 1965. "The Church: Grace upon Grace" studied the link between Christianity and non-Christian religions.

In a lecture entitled "Tradition in Modern Theology," Anscar, then a third-year theology student, defended the theory that "every revealed truth was contained in the Bible at least by allusion, and that Tradition was but an interpretation of the Bible." Some monks called Anscar's statements "heretical."

The lecture was part of a series that the young monks organized and called "Clerics' Modern Mind Lectures." The youthful lecturers spoke on Albert Camus, Odo Casel, Sigmund Freud, and modern music. Reactions were varied, as the audience was composed of junior monks and venerable seniors. During one open forum a rabidly conservative monk asked the speaker whether he had permission to read books that were in the Index. The question was followed by a stunned silence.

After Anscar was ordained priest in 1965, Fr. Bernardo Lopez, who was now abbot, told him that he would be sent to Rome for further studies. Anscar was excited. He wanted to work for a doctorate in systematic theology, but to his disappointment, the abbot wanted him to take a course that would train him to be the abbey's master of ceremonies, a job Anscar detested. In his gentle but uncompromising manner, Abbot Lopez said that he would take the course on liturgy at the Benedictine college. At that time liturgy was mostly rubrics and seemed to be light-years away from theology. Anscar tried to bargain. Could he take theology and some courses in liturgy? The abbot said no. Could he take liturgy and some courses in theology? Again the abbot said no. He should take only liturgy and nothing else. Although it pained him, Anscar obeyed. Now he says with a smile that sometimes superiors can be right.

Anscar studied at the Pontifical Liturgical Institute at Sant' Anselmo from 1965 to 1969. He was in Rome when Vatican II was solemnly concluded on December 8, 1965. His doctoral thesis was entitled *The Cosmic Elements of Christian Passover.* It would be edited fifteen years later and published with a new title, *Shaping the Easter Feast.* I remember a conversation with Anscar during my early years in the abbey. We were talking about the great celebrations in the Philippines: Christmas and Holy Week. Anscar said that he especially loved Holy Week. He thought it was divinely heroic and majestic. I suppose it was also because of his experience of Holy Week in Cainta and in the abbey.

Like many towns in the Philippines, Cainta observes Holy Week with traditions that are both pious and colorful: flagellants in purple robes; the *senakulo*, a passion play that includes the history of salvation and runs for several evenings; the *pabasa*, the chanting of a metric narration of the passion; the *salubong*, the meeting between the risen Lord and his mother after his resurrection. Anscar's family had a *pabasa* in their house on Holy Thursday, and from the windows of the their living room, one had a good view of the church plaza and the streets where the other customs were staged.

Holy Week in the abbey in the 1950s and 1960s had all the grandeur of the Latin Liturgy, with Gregorian chant, pontifical rituals, and elegant vestments. The abbey's neo-Gothic church, one of the most beautiful in Manila, has paintings on the vaulted ceiling and magnificent Stations of the Cross over the Gothic arches, a splendid setting for the solemn liturgy of Holy Week.

Anscar returned to Manila in 1969 and was given assignments in the abbey and the college. He was appointed prefect of brothers, then prefect of clerics, and served as subprior for two years. At San Beda College he served as chaplain of the College of Arts and Sciences and the grade school. He was chair of the Theology Department and professor of theology. He served briefly as chairman of the Board of Trustees of SBC. As college chaplain, he was in charge of the Student Catholic Action. He organized and supervised the apostolate of the students, which was visiting a squatter community just behind the college campus, giving religious instruction to the children, and helping the community by doing manual work. When the squatters were evicted, the students helped them dismantle their shanties. It was a tearful farewell when they left, for they had become good friends with Anscar and the students.

While working in San Beda College, Anscar was a professor of liturgy at San Carlos Major Seminary of the Archdiocese of Manila. In 1972, when six of the professors who belonged to the Congregation of the Immaculate Heart of Mary were relieved of their assignments, Anscar joined them when they founded the Maryhill School of Theology. In 1973, Anscar was surprised to receive a letter from the Abbot

Primate of the Benedictine Confederation inviting him to teach at the Pontifical Liturgical Institute. Anscar gladly accepted the invitation, but Maryhill also wanted him to continue teaching. Fortunately, it was not difficult to arrange. Anscar taught in Rome from October to May, and at Maryhill from June to September, which was the summer vacation in Rome. Some years he returned early enough to spend Holy Week in Manila.

Noting the growing interest in liturgy, even among laypeople, he organized the National Liturgy Week, which was held in Easter Week from 1983 to 1991 at San Beda College. The large number of participants was very encouraging. Priests, religious, and laypeople came from all over the country to attend the lectures.

In 1990, on the recommendation of the Catholic Bishops Conference of the Philippines, the Benedictine abbey founded the Paul VI Institute of Liturgy in Malaybalay, Bukidnon. Anscar was named director. The first group of students included two Chinese priests from Beijing. It was a good omen. Since it opened, the institute has drawn students from the People's Republic of China, Malaysia, Indonesia, Korea, Pakistan, Sri Lanka, Hong Kong, Micronesia, Sweden, Holland, and the United States.

Anscar's reputation as an authority on liturgy, particularly liturgical inculturation, has taken him all over the world, to several cities in the United States, to Russia, China, Germany, Switzerland, Portugal, Zaire, Israel, Samoa, Fiji, New Zealand, New Guinea, and the Bahamas. But nowadays travel and its tight schedules make him more eager to return to the cool air, slower pace, quiet surroundings, and relative isolation of Malaybalay.

People who are awed by his accomplishments are delighted to discover that he is affable, down-to-earth, and easy to like. He is graciously witty, even-tempered, relaxed in manner, and interested in everything. He is calmly organized and enviably systematic, and the best proof of this is his room—every room he has occupied in his migratory life—which is gleamingly clean and orderly. Anscar loves good food—from his mother's home cooking to the haute cuisine he sometimes gets when he travels. While he enjoys Chinese and Italian food, he reserves his highest accolades for a good steak. "Medium rare," he tells the waiter, "but more rare than medium." Nothing, he says, beats the Florentine steak broiled over coals of pine wood.

Anscar has a collection of compact discs that reflects his personality. He loves classical music, from Bach and Vivaldi to Rachmaninoff and Samuel Barber, symphonies, opera, art songs, and chamber music, but he especially enjoys listening to Russian Orthodox chants, with their stately melodies and rich harmonies, and the solemnly resonant voices of the choir and the soloists. I have yet to catch him listening to popular music.

For a person who spends a lot of time reading and writing scholarly works, Anscar manages to read novels. On long plane trips, he brings along several books, and when he comes home, passes them on to anyone who cares to have them. Aside from novels, Anscar reads humorous works which he also passes on. The best ones in my collection are from him. I always look forward to Anscar's return from a trip because I know that he will have new jokes to tell. His jokes are usually very funny and, better still, liturgical.

Cassian Folsom, O.S.B.

Anscar Chupungco and the Pontifical Liturgical Institute (1974–97)

In 1968 Anscar Chupungco completed his doctoral thesis at the Pontifical Liturgical Institute of Sant' Anselmo, entitled *The Cosmic Elements of Christian Passover,* under the direction of Fr. Burkhard Neunheuser, O.S.B., who was *Preside* at the time. Thereupon he returned to his monastery in Manila to take up various duties both in the monastery itself and the school. In 1973 Sant' Anselmo, in the person of Fr. Burkhard Neunheuser, was knocking at his door, inviting him back to Rome to teach at his *alma mater.*

THE INVITATION FROM SANT' ANSELMO (1973–74)
In response to this request, Fr. Chupungco agreed to come and teach temporarily: initially for one year. Some months later, the Abbot Primate, the Most Rev. Rembert Weakland, O.S.B., wrote to Fr. Anscar with an official invitation, saying:

"[The dean and faculty] recognize your competence in the field and realize the importance of having a truly universal faculty which would reflect the universality of the Church herself. As the first Filipino on our faculty, your experience in that country and part of the world should bring a new dimension to studies here where so many students are now coming from the Third World."[1]

Fr. Anscar was pleased at the invitation, but the situation at home required him to stay in Manila some months longer. He wrote to Fr. Neunheuser explaining that because of the antipodal calendar of

1. PIL Archives, Chupungco file, letter (October 9, 1973) of Rembert Weakland to Anscar Chupungco.

their academic year and because of an upcoming visitation of the monastery, he could not come to Rome as soon as had been hoped.

From the very beginning, Fr. Chupungco was caught between two places: between the Philippines and Rome, between the local church and the universal Church. This creative tension was to mark both his life and his scholarship. One of the courses he accepted to teach was a course on "Liturgical Adaptation (Theology and Pastoral Suggestions)." In this way, he identified early what would become his area of expertise.

Since Fr. Anscar made a good impression, the authorities of Sant' Anselmo were anxious to keep him, and during the summer of 1974, the Abbot Primate applied the full weight of his authority in order to have the prior of Manila release Fr. Anscar for an initial period of three years. He arrived as a full-time faculty member in October 1974.

THE BEGINNING YEARS AS A PROFESSOR IN THE LITURGICAL INSTITUTE (1974–77)

The documentation for Anscar Chupungco's activity in this early period is rather scarce. He is listed in the *Liber Annualis* as teaching the course on the History of the Liturgy, a course he was to retain for almost twenty years. During the summers, he would return to the Philippines to teach and give lectures in various places. He began to direct a few license theses at the Liturgical Institute during this period, a work that would greatly increase in subsequent years. He published his doctoral dissertation in *Studia Anselmiana* in 1977, the first of many books to come. In addition, there was already some indication of his organizational and administrative skills: the minutes of the faculty meeting of December 12, 1974, are signed by him; they are clear, orderly, and precise. On March 8, 1975, Neunheuser was reelected *Preside* for a three-year term. In the years 1975–78, Fr. Burkhard was confronted with various challenges having to do with the ongoing stability of the Institute. Two crucial areas of concern emerge from the available documentation: the renewal of the *corpo docente* by the addition of new members, and the relative independence of Liturgical Institute vis-à-vis the theological faculty of Sant' Anselmo. The problem of maintaining a highly qualified faculty, especially full-time Benedictine faculty members, has been a perennial preoccupation of the Liturgical Institute, but apparently in that particular period the problem was more acute than usual. As for the second item, Fr. Anscar, in his history of the Liturgical Institute, reports that: "[t]he juridical status of the Liturgical Institute was a belabored issue from the moment it was established in 1961 until its elevation to the status of a Faculty on 23 August 1978."[2] The very presence of Fr. Anscar at Sant' Anselmo was a response to the first problem: that of maintaining a sufficient number of Benedictines on the faculty. There is evidence that he made a significant contribution to the resolution of the second problem as well, by working for the erection of the Liturgical Institute as a separate faculty. On December 2, 1977, he wrote an impassioned letter to Fr. Neunheuser, which is worth quoting at some length, since it gives an insight into Fr. Chupungco's character and his dedication to the Liturgical Institute.

"In the four years I have been here as a professor I have always had a tormenting anxiety that one day the Institute would be nothing more than a specialization or a faculty of the Ateneo S. Anselmo, always subject to the whims and dispositions of people who are not within the structure of the Institute. I always had the sensation that we are not stable enough, that our orientation which I have loved so much and promoted would have to change because of external pressures. . . . The news, therefore, regarding the independence of the PIL, like the Biblicum, has given me a fresh and renewed desire to continue my work as professor of the Institute. After 17 years of existence, the PIL is no longer merely a branch of the Benedictine Order, nor merely a part of the Ateneo S. Anselmo, but an instrument of the Catholic Church for the promotion of the liturgy as outlined by Vatican II. . . . [N]ow it is clear that the PIL must take on a new image. And as I said before, much of this is on shoulders that a dedicated man like you possess. Father, my only desire is that you will do all in your power to push this plan of the Holy Father and the Congregation into its final realization. We have not got much time. If this is not realized now, I fear that the PIL for which you sacrificed much of yourself shall have been a historical anecdote, something that died because we did not take the signs of the times into account at the acceptable time."[3]

This letter shows Fr. Chupungco's sense of timing, his intuitive feel for organization and administration, and above all his awareness of the importance of the structural foundations of institutional government.

2. Anscar Chupungco, "The Pontifical Liturgical Institute: A Benedictine Service to the Church," *Ecclesia Orans* (1987) 35.
3. PIL Archives, Chupungco file, letter (December 2, 1977) of Anscar Chupungco to Burkhard Neunheuser.

When Burkhard Neunheuser's term of office came to an end in March 1978, these outstanding qualities made the young professor an obvious candidate for *Preside*.

FIRST TERM AS *PRESIDE* (MARCH 1978–FEBRUARY 1981)
On March 16, 1978, Anscar Chupungco was elected as the third *Preside* of the Liturgical Institute. Fr. Neunheuser wrote in the margin of his personal notes: *quem Ds adiuvet!* A month later, on April 15, 1978, Fr. Anscar presided at his first faculty meeting, in which he immediately established the tone of his administration. While acknowledging that he was among the youngest of the faculty members, he expressed his confidence in the wisdom and experience of the *corpo docente* and invited the collaboration of all in the great work that lay ahead. Indeed there was much work to be done. Just a few months earlier (January 1978) the Grand Chancellor, the Most Rev. Victor Dammertz, O.S.B., had officially written to the Holy See requesting that the Liturgical Institute be granted the status of a separate and distinct faculty; one of the consequences of the new status would be that the PIL would be able to grant academic degrees in its own name. At the time of the April faculty meeting, the response had not yet come back from the Congregation for Catholic Education, but an affirmative answer was assured. This important change in the status of the Institute would have a domino effect, requiring changes in the Statutes and the Procedural Norms.

Fr. Chupungco's genius for good administration was already manifesting itself. He announced a revision of the curriculum which would have a lasting effect on the program of studies: a two-year cycle of courses beginning in the year 1979–80. He also indicated the need for a reorganization of the office of the *Preside*, especially in terms of putting the archives in order and preparing a list of the license and doctoral dissertations written in the first sixteen years of the Institute's history. As any good administrator, Fr. Chupungco was concerned with the financial stability of the school. By establishing contact with various benefactors, he was able to announce a program of student scholarships, the establishment of a seminar room for student research, and the acquisition of audiovisual equipment for classroom use and microfilm/microfiche materials for the library. The April fifteenth meeting set high goals for the Liturgical Institute and at the same time gave the faculty the assurance that those high goals would be competently met.

In the same semester of the 1977–78 academic year, Anscar Chupungco was appointed Vice-Rector, named a consultor to the Sacred Congregation for the Sacraments and Divine Worship, and was promoted to the rank of professor *straordinarius*.[4] He began to carry through on the many projects that had been announced, adding to the already existing structures a new commission for overseeing the scholarly publications of the Institute.

In his first term of office, Fr. Chupungco would work on many fronts at the same time. Some can be summarized briefly: inviting new professors, carrying out the curriculum revision, putting into writing the various procedures for the registrar's office, the library, the student government, and the school's publications. Other projects require a longer explanation: the work on the Statutes; attempts to find economic stability for the Institute; protracted negotiations with affiliate institutions; and the establishment of a rhythm of symposia, punctuated from time to time by a new initiative, the international liturgical congress.

The importance of the revision of the Statutes was not only to establish clear structures and procedures for the good administration of the Institute, but also to articulate the purpose for which the Institute was established. The "Mission Statement" was formulated in three paragraphs:

a. to promote the progress of liturgical studies, both by the scientific research of the teachers, and the formation of select students who can devote themselves to scientific studies,
b. to prepare teachers in the scientific method, who will be able to teach the discipline of liturgical studies in universities, faculties, seminaries, and religious houses,
c. to prepare experts to work for regional and diocesan liturgical commissions, as well as animators who render an important service in pastoral liturgy.[5]

Creative efforts to provide for the financial stability of the institution were not lacking during Fr. Chupungco's first term of office. The most interesting attempt, which ultimately came to naught, was connected with the change in the Institute's status as a separate faculty

4. The various stages of faculty rank and promotion in the Roman system are: *lector, consociatus, straordinarius, ordinarius*.
5. Chupungco, "The Pontifical Liturgical Institute," 30.

(which took place in 1978). Apparently, in the academic year 1977–78, Pope Paul VI let it be known that the Holy See intended to create a fund for the Liturgical Institute, to be administered by the Cardinal Prefect of the Congregation for the Sacraments and Divine Worship, who would also serve as the Cardinal Patron of the Institute. In fact, the papal donation was originally intended to be included in the document which raised the Institute to the level of a faculty in its own right. However, with the death of Pope Paul VI in August 1978, the sudden death of Pope John Paul I in September, and the election of Pope John Paul II in October, the situation radically changed, and the document was issued without mention either of the pontifical donation or the cardinalate patronage.[6]

One of the administrative items that consumed a great deal of energy during Fr. Anscar's first term was the long and difficult negotiation with an affiliate school, the Institute of Pastoral Liturgy in Padova. The history of the relationship between Sant'Anselmo and Padova is too long and complex to go into here. Suffice it to say that in 1977 a five-year trial period was agreed upon, requiring the active involvement of PIL faculty members in the teaching at Padova, while the *Preside* was much involved in negotiating the academic and canonical status of the relationship. In this area also, Anscar Chupungco's administrative skills were put to the test.

One of Fr. Anscar's initiatives which allowed the Liturgical Institute to present itself to the larger academic and ecclesiastical world, was the establishment of a steady rhythm of symposia and faculty study days: from 1978 onward, these were held practically every semester. "It was felt, however," Chupungco later recorded, "that the Liturgical Institute had to show evidence of its international character. Symposia are usually a Roman or at most Italian affair, as far as participation is concerned."[7] So starting in November 1980, plans were made for the First International Liturgy Congress, scheduled for May of 1982.

In the midst of all this intense administrative activity, Fr. Anscar continued the normal round of teaching and writing. In this period he directed nine license theses and four doctoral dissertations.

6. PIL Archives, *Verbali del Consiglio dell'Istituto,* meeting of November 29, 1979.
7. Chupungco, "The Pontifical Liturgical Institute," 47.

SECOND TERM AS *PRESIDE* (FEBRUARY 1981–JANUARY 1985)
The election took place on January 22, 1981, and Fr. Chupungco was elected by an overwhelming majority. A few months later, on April 4, 1981, he was raised to the rank of *ordinarius;* this promotion acknowledged his academic competence and his contribution to the field of liturgical studies. The addition of a new professor *ordinarius* was also part of the ongoing effort to maintain and increase the stability of the PIL faculty. The second term of Fr. Chupungco as *Preside* was a period of continuity and consolidation as well as a time of important new initiatives.

Projects begun during the first term were carried over into the second: curriculum adjustments; publications; work on statutes, procedural norms, and special regulations; the 1982 international congress, as well as regular symposia; and continued negotiations with the Institute of Pastoral Liturgy in Padova.

The manual of liturgical studies, *Anàmnesis,* begun in 1972 under the direction of the first president of the Liturgical Institute, Salvatore Marsili, had a long and rather gradual history. By the time of Fr. Marsili's death in 1983, only two volumes had been published, while the third volume, on the sacraments, was still in the preparation stages. At the first faculty meeting of the 1984–85 school year, Fr. Chupungco announced that he would take over the editorship of the manual. During his second term, he coaxed this third volume along, and saw it published in 1983. During this period several other publication projects were brought to completion: a *miscellanea* in honor of Fr. Marsili, another in honor of Fr. Adrien Nocent, and the publication of the *Acta* of the First International Liturgical Congress. In November 1984, in order to give a new and structured impetus to the whole area of publications, Fr. Anscar began to work on new regulations for the Publications Commission, thus manifesting once again his gift for giving structural form to what had previously been a matter of individual initiative.

In preparation for the First International Liturgical Congress on the topic of *The Symbols of Christian Initiation,* all the behind-the-scenes work was carefully orchestrated, including the necessary fund raising. As a result, everything was ready for May 24–28, 1982, and the grand success of the event led to the establishment of an ongoing tradition of international congresses, usually held every three years. In fact, plans began right away for the Second International Congress scheduled for 1985 on the theme of Christian Marriage. Meanwhile smaller-scale symposia continued on a more frequent basis.

In addition to maintaining the existing levels of activity, several new initiatives were launched during Fr. Chupungco's second term. In the faculty meeting of March 3, 1984, plans were made for creating an association of professors of liturgy and sacraments from the various Roman athenaea. The meetings of the first few years were quite fruitful. In 1983 a newsletter was begun for the PIL alumni, printed in both Italian and English. Although this did not last more than a year or so, it was a harbinger of future efforts in the area of development, and was a creative response to a genuine need.

An initiative particularly characteristic of Fr. Chupungco's style was the granting of the doctorate *honoris causa* to liturgists of particular stature or merit, often on a special occasion, such as the celebration of the twenty-fifth anniversary of the Liturgical Institute in conjunction with the Second International Liturgical Congress in May 1985. The granting of these academic honors not only recognized the outstanding contribution of well-known liturgists, but also manifested the Liturgical Institute's involvement with the world of liturgical studies at the highest academic and ecclesiastical levels.

By far the most important initiative taken during Fr. Chupungco's second term was the founding of the scholarly journal *Ecclesia Orans* in February 1984. Already in 1981 there had been some tentative moves in the direction of a collaborative effort with the liturgical journal *Questions Liturgiques,* but the project never materialized and in 1982 the idea was put on hold. A year later, there was renewed discussion of the question, this time with the proposal that the Liturgical Institute itself begin a scholarly journal.

Thus, by January of 1985, at the completion of Fr. Chupungco's second term in office, the Liturgical Institute was thriving. During this period, in addition to administering, teaching, and writing, Fr. Anscar was also the director of some twenty-five license theses and four doctoral theses.

THIRD TERM AS *PRESIDE* (JANUARY–NOVEMBER 1985)
According to the Statutes of the Liturgical Institute, the *Preside* can be elected for no more than two consecutive terms. In the election of January 25, 1985, therefore, Fr. Chupungco was not eligible. Due to the esteem in which he was held, however, and the small number of other qualified candidates, Fr. Anscar was postulated for a third term. The life and work of the Institute continued as before, the most note-

worthy event being the Second International Liturgical Congress on the Christian Celebration of Marriage (May 27–31, 1985).

The atmosphere of "business as usual" was to be short-lived, however, because a few short months later, at the beginning of the academic year 1985–86, another election was held, this time for the *Rettore Magnifico* of the entire Athenaeum of Sant' Anselmo (embracing the three faculties of philosophy, theology, and liturgy). On November 14, 1985, Fr. Chupungco was elected rector by an overwhelming majority. While this was a gain for the Athenaeum as a whole, it was a loss for the Liturgical Institute, and preparations had to be made for the election of a new *Preside*. On December 12, 1985, the very affable professor Fr. Ildebrando Scicolone, O.S.B., was postulated as the new president, his term going into effect on February 17, 1986, at the beginning of the second semester. On January 16, 1986, Fr. Chupungco convened the last meeting he would have with the faculty in his capacity as *Preside*.

AS *RETTORE MAGNIFICO* (NOVEMBER 1985–DECEMBER 1989)

As Rector, Fr. Chupungco's energies were obviously dedicated to the Athenaeum as a whole, and he was therefore less involved than he had been in the daily operations of the Liturgical Institute. Nevertheless, he remained a very active figure in the life of the Institute. In the first place, he taught his usual classes, continued his research and writing, and during this time period, directed twelve license theses and seven doctoral dissertations. According to the revised Statutes of the Athenaeum, the rector automatically becomes a member of the Dean's Council of whatever faculty he is a member of; this meant that Fr. Chupungco became a member of the *Consiglio del Preside* of the PIL, and thus served as one of the president's advisors. Fr. Anscar remained the editor of *Anàmnesis* and during his term as Rector two volumes were published: one in 1986, the other in 1988. In March of 1986, Fr. Chupungco was elected a member of the Publications Committee of the Liturgical Institute (as *Preside* he had been an *ex officio* member; now he was a member by election). In addition, he served as coeditor (along with Giustino Farnedi) for the Miscellanea in honor of Fr. Nocent. During this time, he did not cease to look out for the financial stability of the Liturgical Institute. Through the mediation of Mons. Anton Hänggi, retired bishop of Basel and doctor *honoris causa* of the PIL, *Missio München* gave a sizeable donation to the Sant' Anselmo library for acquisitions in the liturgical section of the

Athenaeum's holdings. In the meetings of the PIL faculty, Fr. Chupungco remained an active participant. In November 1988 he proposed a postdoctoral program for PIL alumni, whereby former students would be able to return to Sant'Anselmo for a kind of refresher course of continuing education. While the project never actually materialized, the proposal itself shows Fr. Chupungco's continued interest in the vitality of the Institute.

Certain initiatives which Fr. Chupungco undertook on behalf of the entire Athenaeum also benefited the Liturgical Institute in a particular way. For example, after a hiatus of over ten years, he reinstituted the publication of the *Liber Annualis,* a useful document prepared by the Registrar's Office which recounts the special events of the Athenaeum, details the activities and publications of the professors, provides a directory of the students and lists the doctoral theses defended in the academic year in question.

During Fr. Anscar's term as rector, Sant' Anselmo celebrated the centenary of its founding with a yearlong series of special events beginning March 20–21, 1987, and extending to the close of the academic year 1987–88. The specific contribution of the Liturgical Institute was the Third International Congress held from May 9–13, 1988, on the topic: "The Celebration of the Paschal Triduum: Anamnesis and Mimesis."

The academic year 1989–90 began smoothly. The Rector's Address (October 16, 1989) which inaugurated the new school year was "vintage Chupungco": describing the accomplishments of the previous year and looking ahead to the challenges of the year to come. The Athenaeum was *totum in pace compositum,* as it would later be described,[8] although two important elections were scheduled for December: the election of the rector on December 3 and the election of the *Preside* on December 7, but the common expectation was that both incumbents would simply be reelected. Suddenly, at the end of October, Fr. Chupungco announced that he would no longer be able to remain full-time at Sant' Anselmo, since his community in Manila along with the Episcopal Conference of the Philippines had requested and required his services at home in order to found an institute of liturgical formation for the local church in the Philippines. This unexpected announcement created a domino effect, in which many of the major administrative posts at Sant'Anselmo had to be

8. "Cronica," *Ecclesia Orans* 3 (1986) 116.

changed. In the election of December 3, 1989, Fr. Pius Tragan, dean of the Theology faculty, was elected rector.

The Grand Chancellor, the Most Rev. Victor Dammertz, O.S.B., while somewhat taken aback by the suddenness of Fr. Anscar's announcement, expressed his appreciation in similar terms:

"At the time when Fr. Chupungco leaves the office of *Rettore Magnifico* to return home for the direct service of his community and the Church of the Philippines by founding a school of liturgical formation there, this is a fitting occasion for expressing to him our gratitude for all the good he has done for our Athenaeum, as professor for seventeen years, as *Preside* for eight years, and as *Rettore Magnifico* for four years."[9]

Thus Fr. Anscar left Sant'Anselmo on February 18, 1990, to found the Paul VI Institute of Liturgy in his beloved homeland.

PAUL VI INSTITUTE (JANUARY 1990–NOVEMBER 1993)
For the four years extending from 1990 to 1993, Fr. Chupungco's presence at Sant' Anselmo was necessarily limited. Each year he returned for a condensed period of time (usually October to Christmas) to teach his courses on the history of the liturgy and inculturation. During this period he sharply reduced his workload as thesis director, however, making sure that six license theses being written under his direction were completed in the 1989–90 academic year; one more was completed a year later. The same pattern holds for doctoral theses: five dissertations for which he was moderator were defended in 1989–90, and one each in 1990–91 and 1991–92. The Fourth International Liturgical Congress was held in Rome from May 6–10, 1991, on the topic "The Cultural Adaptation of the Liturgy." Since this is Fr. Chupungco's area of specialization, he not only delivered several addresses to the Congress, but was also involved in the behind-the-scenes work of preparation.

As director of the Paul VI Institute of Liturgy in the Philippines, Fr. Chupungco naturally increased his activity in the local church. In the 1991–92 school year he was named secretary of the National Liturgical Commission of the Philippines. In March 1991, as part of his work

9. *Liber Annualis* (1988–89): Cover letter from the Most Rev. Victor Dammertz, O.S.B. (February 18, 1990), dedicating the 1988–89 edition of the *Liber Annualis* to Anscar J. Chupungco.

to establish the Paul VI Institute on solid footing, he requested the *patrocinium* of the Pontifical Liturgical Institute so as to grant a (non-academic) diploma under the auspices of the PIL to those completing their studies in the Filipino Institute.

During this same time period, certain events were taking place which would have a considerable impact on the Pontifical Liturgical Institute. The Congress of Benedictine Abbots meeting from September 15–25, 1992, concerned with certain difficulties in the *Collegio* and the Athenaeum of Sant'Anselmo, elected Abbot Jerome Theisen of St. John's Abbey in Collegeville, Minnesota, as Abbot Primate, because—among other reasons—of his experience in administering a large academic institution. The same Congress of Abbots appointed a Special Commission for Sant'Anselmo, with the mandate to assist the Athenaeum in maintaining and improving its academic program. The Liturgical Institute needed this special assistance especially because of the extremely low number of full-time Benedictines on the faculty. On November 4, 1993, the Grand Chancellor, Jerome Theisen, nominated Fr. Chupungco as *Pro-Preside* for an indefinite period, to coincide with the time needed by the Special Commission for Sant' Anselmo to do its work, and possibly extending to the next Congress of Abbots scheduled for September 1996. This solution was clearly a temporary one, because when Fr. Chupungco accepted this new assignment, he did not cease to be director of the Paul VI Institute in the Philippines. The fact that the two institutes were in session in two different periods made the arrangement possible, but there were times when the two calendars inevitably overlapped, necessitating Fr. Chupungco's absence from one or the other.

PRO-PRESIDE (DECEMBER 1993–MARCH 1997)

Fr. Chupungco immediately took the situation in hand. In his first faculty meeting, January 15, 1994, he laid out his threefold program of action: to reinvigorate the faculty, reform the process of admissions, and renew the program of studies. Building on the foundation laid by the previous administration, Fr. Chupungco laid out a strategy for faculty development. He was able to arrange for a long-time and highly qualified part-time professor to transfer his tenured status from another university to the Liturgical Institute. He made sure that the younger faculty members, both Benedictine and non-Benedictine, were promoted at regular intervals according to their years of teaching experience and their publications. He was able to obtain the services of several new full-time teachers, and started them out on the long road of faculty promotion in the tenure track. As a result the *corpo docente* regained a certain stability although, on account of the generation gap caused by the loss of personnel, the faculty remains rather young.

Fr. Chupungco also addressed the problem of admission standards. Because of the decline of educational standards in many countries and because of the lack of adequate preparation in classical languages in many seminaries, the Liturgical Institute needed to clarify what its expectations were, especially in the area of Latin.

The question of a curriculum revision had already been under discussion for some time, and action in this area was mandated by the Special Commission for Sant' Anselmo. Fr. Chupungco established a new committee to move the issue forward, and began the laborious process of discussions and meetings in order to come up with a concrete proposal to submit to the faculty. In the meantime, Fr. Chupungco made certain minor modifications in the existing program, in particular by organizing the optional courses into a regular cycle, so as to allow students the possibility of covering the major questions of pastoral liturgy within a two-year period.

Perhaps the best example of Fr. Chupungco's creative genius was an exciting new initiative, proposed already in the second faculty meeting of March 3, 1994, of a new five-volume manual of liturgical studies to replace the by now-outdated series *Anàmnesis*. Fr. Anscar applied himself to the planning of this new venture with great enthusiasm, and in the final faculty meeting of the 1993–94 academic year was able to present the criteria to be used in the organization and structure of the new manual. The work of the professors on their respective articles for the new manual galvanized the faculty as a whole, and contributed to a new creative spirit. The weight of the editorial work fell to Fr. Chupungco himself, who appointed a special assistant, Fr. Adam Somorjai, O.S.B., to help him with this task.

Also in the area of publications, Fr. Chupungco made contact with the editors of the Herder publishing house to reprint several important liturgical books in Sant' Anselmo's *Rerum Ecclesiasticarum Documenta* series, which had been out of print for some time. He also worked to strengthen *Ecclesia Orans*.

When Fr. Chupungco was appointed as *Pro-Preside* in November 1993 he had to make a difficult decision concerning the Fifth International Liturgical Congress on the theme of "Confirmation," scheduled for May 1994. Because of the enormous amount of work to be done at the beginning of his mandate, and on account of the reduced number of people available to do the work, Fr. Chupungco decided to cancel the congress. The question of rescheduling the congress was put on hold for some time, and reintroduced in a faculty meeting of November 16, 1995, but the moment was not ripe and other more urgent concerns relegated the congress to the background for the time being. A successful two-day symposium was held on May 4–5, 1995, on the Hebrew Sabbath, but the normal rhythm of symposia and congresses customary in earlier years was yet unable to be reestablished.

There were other signs of new vitality, however. Fr. Chupungco arranged for a number of doctorates *honoris causa* to be granted, thus polishing the Institute's public image. He also welcomed a proposal to inaugurate a new continuing education course on Thursday evenings: "Architecture and the Arts for the Liturgy." A related initiative was the granting of *patrocinium* to the *Scuola Beato Angelico* in Milan: an institute dedicated to practical training in the many arts used in the liturgy.

During these years, Fr. Chupungco was in very great demand as a thesis director. From the fall of 1993 to the spring of 1997 he directed twenty-three license theses and six doctoral dissertations. It was also a time for receiving significant honors from other academic institutions. In 1996 Fr. Chupungco received two honorary doctorates: one from the Ateneo de Manila University in the Philippines, the other from the Catholic Theological Union at Chicago.

During these challenging years, Fr. Chupungco's generosity of service could not hide the wear and tear on him personally caused by having to administer two institutes simultaneously in different parts of the world. Furthermore, the *Pro-Preside* was unfortunately obliged to be absent at rather key moments of the academic year: the beginning and end of each semester. Once stability was reestablished in the Pontifical Liturgical Institute, therefore, Fr. Chupungco began to look for ways to normalize the situation. As the chronicle records:

"After almost four years of serving as *Pro-Preside ad nutum abbatis*, Fr. Anscar Chupungco asked the Grand Chancellor, the Most Rev. Marcel Rooney, O.S.B., to be relieved of this office so that he could dedicate himself more completely to the Paul VI Institute of Liturgy which he had founded in the Philippines. Father Abbot Primate, in his capacity as Grand Chancellor, acceded to Fr. Chupungco's request, and in late February, in accord with the directives of the special Commission for Sant' Anselmo established by the Abbots' Congress in 1992, appointed Fr. Cassian Folsom, O.S.B., as *Pro-Preside* in his place."[10]

Since Fr. Folsom had worked closely with Fr. Chupungco, especially since the 1995–96 academic year, the transition in administration was smooth, demonstrating both the continuity of the Liturgical Institute's tradition and its adaptability to new circumstances. Thus Fr. Chupungco did a yeoman's service, and at long last was granted a well-earned sabbatical period in reward for his many labors.

* * *

As of this writing, Fr. Anscar J. Chupungco has served the Pontifical Liturgical Institute for twenty-three years as professor, twelve years as *Preside/Pro-Preside* and four years as rector of the Athenaeum of Sant' Anselmo: an extraordinary record by any standard of measurement. His personal activity during this period included teaching, directing student theses, writing books and articles, and lecturing in various parts of the world. Fr. Chupungco is an extraordinary administrator, and his contribution to the Liturgical Institute is permanent and enduring. In one of my last conversations with him in Rome, during a period of intense activity, I asked him why he did everything that he was doing. He answered very simply, "Because I love the Institute."

---

10. "Cronica," *Ecclesia Orans* 14 (1997) 326.

CATHOLIC THEOLOGICAL UNION
ANSCAR J. CHUPUNGCO, O.S.B.
DOCTOR OF THEOLOGY, *honoris causa*

Since its foundation in the midst of the liturgical reform of the 1960s, Catholic Theological Union has always recognized the crucial importance of the liturgy in enacting the renewed vision of Church proclaimed by the Second Vatican Council. Ongoing liturgical renewal continues to be an area of vital interest to the school as it prepares students to minister throughout the world in a multitude of cultural contexts.

These twin concerns of liturgical reform and the cultural expression of faith have impassioned the man we honor today. Father Anscar Chupungco, O.S.B., is recognized as the preeminent Roman Catholic expert on liturgical inculturation. The relationship of liturgy to its cultural context figures prominently in practically all of his writings. In his many books and articles, Fr. Anscar has consistently wedded a profound knowledge of the worship tradition of the Church with keen insights into establishing theological criteria for the inculturation of the liturgy.

In addition to being a prolific writer and respected teacher, he is founder and present director of Paul VI Institute of Liturgy in the Philippines. Former president of the Pontifical Liturgical Institute and Rector Magnificus of the Pontifical Athenaeum of Sant' Anselmo in Rome, he is also a valued consultant, having served organizations as diverse as two Vatican Congregations, the International Commission on English in the Liturgy, the World Council of Churches and the Lutheran World Federation. He is also executive secretary of the Episcopal Commission on Liturgy in the Philippines as well as Regional Secretary for South East Asia of the Asian Liturgy Forum.

But in all of these varied activities, Fr. Anscar, a loyal son of Benedict, has sought to share with the wider Church the monastic insistence that common worship is an encounter with the living God and not simply a recitation of texts. Much of his concern for inculturation of the liturgy can be summed up in the monastic saying, *si cor non orat in vana lingua laborat.* Through his teaching, writing, work of administration and consultation, he has made real liturgical prayer possible for hearts throughout the world.

Therefore, it is with gratitude for his outstanding contribution to the liturgical renewal of the Church that the Faculty and the Board of Trustees of Catholic Theological Union confer upon Anscar J. Chupungco, O.S.B. the Degree of

DOCTOR OF THEOLOGY, *honoris causa*

Given at Chicago, in the State of Illinois,

The 5th Day of June, 1997

Donald Senior, C.P., President

Bibliography of Anscar J. Chupungco, O.S.B.

"An Essay on Symbolism and Liturgical Celebration," *Symbolisme et Théologie*, Studia Anselmiana 64 (Roma: Anselmiana, 1974) 173–93.

Towards a Filipino Liturgy (Manila: Benedictine Abbey, 1976).

"Filipino Culture and Christian Liturgy," *Lit. Cult.* (1977) 62–71.

The Cosmic Elements of Christian Passover, Studia Anselmiana 72, Analecta Liturgica 3, Pontificium Institutum Liturgicum: Pars Dissertationis ad Doctoratum in S. Liturgia (Roma: Anselmiana, 1977).

"A Filipino Attempt at Liturgical Indigenization," *Ephemerides Liturgicae* 91 (1977) 370–76.

"Verso una liturgia per le Filippine," *Rivista liturgica* 65 (1978) 144–49.

"Talasalitaang—Liturhiko—Pastoral," *Maryhill Studies* 1 (S.L.: Maryhill, 1978).

"A Filipino Adaptation of the Liturgical Language," *Eulogia: miscellanea liturgica in onore di P. Burkhard Neunheuser, OSB, preside del Pontificio Istituto Liturgico*, Studia Anselmiana 68 (Roma: Anselmiana, 1979) 45–55.

Liturgical Renewal in the Philippines, ed. Anscar J. Chupungco, Maryhill Studies 3 (S.L.: Maryhill, 1980).

"Liturgical Feasts and Seasons of the Year," *The Times of Celebration*, ed. David Power, *Concilium* (New York: The Seabury Press, 1981) 31–36.

"A Historical Survey of Liturgical Adaptation," *Notitiae* 17 (1981) 28–43.

"The English Translation of the Liturgy," *Notitiae* 18 (1982) 91–100.

"Fifteen Years after the Instruction *Eucharisticum Mysterium*," *Notitiae* 18 (1982) 281–86.

Cultural Adaptation of the Liturgy (New York: Paulist Press, 1982).

"The Sacred Liturgy: The Unfinished Task," *Remembering the Future: Vatican II and Tomorrow's Liturgical Agenda*, ed. Carl Last (New York: Paulist Press, 1983) 80–99.

"L'adattamento liturgico nell'Ordo Missae: principi e possibilità," *Anàmnesis: Introduzione storico-teologica alla liturgia*, Vol. 3/2. *La liturgia, eucaristia: teologia e storia della celebrazione,* ed. by Salvatore Marsili (Casale Monferrato: Marietti, 1983) 289–317.

"On the Twenty-first Anniversary of the Pontifical Liturgical Institute," *I simboli dell'iniziazione cristiana,* Studia Anselmiana 87 (Roma: Anselmiana, 1983) 9–12.

"Nel 20 anniversario della *Sacrosanctum Concilium,*" *Notitiae* 19 (1983) 695–707.

"Adaptation of the Liturgy to the Culture and Traditions of the People," *Osservatore Romano* 46 (1984) 7.

"Adaptation de la liturgie à la culture et aux traditions des peuples," *La Maison-Dieu* 162 (1984) 23–30.

"Le texte de Lima indicateur pour le futur: une perspective culturelle," *La Maison-Dieu* 163 (1984) 59–68.

"The Place of Sunday in the Liturgical Year: A Re-reading of SC 106," *Ecclesia Orans* 1 (1984) 133–51.

"Educazione, cultura, evangelizzazione," *Seminarium* 25 (1985) 202–14.

"The Place of Culture in the Study of Liturgy," *Seminarium* 25 (1985) 256–65.

"Adattamento all'indole e alle tradizioni dei vari popoli," *Rivista di pastorale liturgica* 23 (1985) 59–61.

L'adattamento della liturgia tra culture e teologia, trans. Leandro Calvo (Casale Monferrato: Edizioni Piemme, 1985).

"Salvatore Marsili: teologo della liturgia," *Paschale mysterium: studi in memoria dell'Abate Prof. Salvatore Marsili (1910–1983),* ed. Giustino Farnedi, Studia Anselmiana 91 (Roma: Anselmiana, 1986) 15–24.

"Der Sonntag und die Kultur: ein Beitrag zur Feier des Herrentags in den Missionen," *Der Sonntag,* ed. Alberich Altermatt, Thaddäus Schnitker, and W. Heim (Würzburg: Echter Verlag, 1986) 225–35.

"L'adattamento della liturgia dei sacramenti: principi e possibilità," *Anàmnesis: Introduzione storico-teologica alla liturgia,* Vol. 3/1. *La liturgia, i sacramenti: teologia e storia della celbrazione,* ed. Anscar Chupungco (Genova: Marietti, 1986) 365–404.

"The Cultural Adaptation of the Rite of Marriage," *La celebrazione cristiana del matrimonio: simboli e testi,* ed. G. Farnedi, Studia Anselmiana 93 (Roma: Anselmiana, 1986) 145–61.

"The Lima Text as a Pointer for the Future: An Asian Perspective," *Studia Liturgica* 16–17 (1986–87) 100–07.

"The Pontifical Liturgical Institute: A Benedictine Service to the Church," *Ecclesia Orans* 4 (1987) 23–56.

"A Definition of Liturgical Inculturation," *Ecclesia Orans* 5 (1988) 11–23.

"The Adaptation of the Liturgical Year: A Theological Perspective," *Traditio et progressio: studi liturgici in onore di A. Nocent,* ed. G. Farnedi, Studia Anselmiana 95 (Roma: Anselmiana, 1988) 149–61.

"The Pontifical Liturgical Institute: A Benedictine Service to the Church," *Sant'Anselmo: saggi storici e d'attualità,* ed. G. Békés, Studia Anselmiana 97 (Roma: Anselmiana, 1988) 193–226.

"La nuova sede della Biblioteca dell'Ateneo S. Anselmo," *Sant'Anselmo: saggi storici e d'attualità,* ed. G. Békés, Studia Anselmiana 97 (Roma: Anselmiana, 1988) 257–60.

"L'adattamento dell'anno liturgico: principi e possibilità," *Anàmnesis: Introduzione storico-teologica alla liturgia,* Vol. 6. *L'anno liturgico: storia, teoria e celebrazione,* intro. and ed. Anscar Chupungco (Genova: Marietti, 1988) 271–306.

Liturgies of the Future: The Process and Methods of Inculturation (Mahwah, N.J.: Paulist Press, 1989).

"L'adattamento dei sacramentali: principi e possibilità," *Anàmnesis: Introduzione storico-teologica alla liturgia,* Vol. 7. *I sacramentali e le benedizioni,* ed. Ildebrando Scicolone (Genova: Marietti, 1989) 251–65.

"Inculturation and the Organic Progression of the Liturgy," *Ecclesia Orans* 7 (1990) 7–21.

"Anamnesis and Mimesis in the Celebration of Easter Sunday," *La celebrazione del triduo pasquale: anamnesis e mimesis. Atti del III Congresso Internazionale di Liturgia,* Studia Anselmiana 102 (Roma: Anselmiana, 1990) 259–71.

"Popular Religiosity and Liturgical Inculturation," *Ecclesia Orans* 8 (1991) 97–115.

"The Conciliar Discussion on *Veritas Horarum,*" *Ecclesia Orans* 8 (1991) 219–29.

Liturgie del futuro: processo e metodi dell'inculturazione, Dabar: Saggi teologici 43 (Genova: Marietti, 1991).

Liturgical Inculturation: Sacramentals, Religiosity, and Catechesis (Collegeville: The Liturgical Press, 1992).

Shaping the Easter Feast (Washington, D.C.: The Pastoral Press, 1992).

"Toward a Ferial Order of Mass," *Ecclesia Orans* 10 (1993) 11–32.

"Liturgical Inculturation in Multiethnic Churches," *Pastoral Music* 17 (1993) 28–29.

"Revision, Adaptation, and Inculturation: A Definition of Terms," *L'adattamento culturale della liturgia: metodi e modelli,* ed. I. Scicolone, Studia Anselmiana 113 (Roma: Anselmiana, 1993) 13–26.

"The Methods of Liturgical Inculturation," *L'adattamento culturale della liturgia: metodi e modelli*, ed. I. Scicolone, Studia Anselmiana 113 (Roma: Anselmiana, 1993) 187–201.

Worship: Beyond Inculturation (Washington, D.C.: Pastoral Press, 1994). [In 1995, reissued under the title *Worship: Progress and Tradition*.]

"Remarks on 'The Roman Liturgy and Inculturation,'" *Ecclesia Orans* 11 (1994) 269–77.

"Liturgical Inculturation and the Search for Unity," *So We Believe, So We Pray: Towards Koinonia in Worship*, ed. Thomas Best and Dagmar Heller (Faith and Order Paper 171) (Geneva: WWCC Publications, 1995) 55–64.

"Ordination and Theology in the *Apostolic Tradition*," *Mysterium Christi: Symbolgegenwart und Theologische Bedeutung. Festschrift für Basil Studer*, ed. M. Löhrer and E. Salmann, Studia Anselmiana 116 (Roma: Anselmiana, 1995) 107–30.

A Church Caught between Tradition and Progress (Notre Dame, Ind.: Notre Dame Center for Pastoral Liturgy, 1995).

"Inculturazione e liturgia: i termini del problema," *Rivista Liturgica* 82 (1995) 361–85.

Handbook for Liturgical Studies, 5 vols., ed. Anscar J. Chupungo (Collegeville: The Liturgical Press, 1997–).

"A Definition of Liturgy," *Handbook for Liturgical Studies*, ed. Anscar Chupungco (Collegeville: The Liturgical Press, 1997) 1:3–10.

"History of the Liturgy Until the Fourth Century," *Handbook for Liturgical Studies* (Collegeville: The Liturgical Press, 1997) 1:95–113.

"History of the Roman Liturgy Until the Fifteenth Century," *Handbook for Liturgical Studies* (Collegeville: The Liturgical Press, 1997) 1:131–52.

"The Translation of Liturgical Texts," *Handbook for Liturgical Studies* (Collegeville: The Liturgical Press, 1997) 1:381–97.

"Ritual Language and Liturgy," *Finding Voice to Give God Praise*, ed. Kathleen Hughes (Collegeville: The Liturgical Press, 1998) 87–99.

Scientia Liturgica: Manuale di Liturgia, 5 vols., ed. Anscar Chupungco (Casale Monferrato: Piemme, 1998).

"Liturgy and Inculturation," *Handbook for Liturgical Studies* (Collegeville: The Liturgical Press, 1998) 2:337–75.

List of Contributors

The Rev. Cassian Folsom, O.S.B., Pro-Preside of the Pontifical Liturgical Institute of St. Anselm, Rome, Italy.

The Rev. Mark R. Francis, C.S.V., Associate Professor of Liturgy, Catholic Theological Union, Chicago, Illinois.

The Most Rev. Wilton D. Gregory, S.L.D., Bishop of Belleville, Illinois.

Sr. Margaret Mary Kelleher, O.S.U., Associate Professor of Liturgy, Department of Religion and Religious Studies, The Catholic University of America, Washington, D.C.

Dr. Gordon W. Lathrop, Schieren Professor of Liturgy, Lutheran Theological Seminary, Philadelphia.

The Rev. Burkhard Neunheuser, O.S.B., Professor Emeritus of the Pontifical Liturgical Institute, Maria Lach, Germany.

The Rev. Gilbert Ostdiek, O.F.M., Professor of Liturgy, Catholic Theological Union, Chicago, Illinois.

Dr. John R. Page, Executive Secretary, International Commission on English in the Liturgy, Washington, D.C.

The Rev. Keith F. Pecklers, S.J., Professor of Liturgical History, Pontifical Liturgical Institute of St. Anselm, Rome, Italy.

The Rev. Bernardo Ma. Pérez, O.S.B., Rector, San Beda College, Our Lady of Montserrat Monastery, Manila, Philippines.

The Rev. Dominic E. Serra, Associate Professor of Liturgy, St. Paul Seminary, St. Paul, Minnesota.

The Rev. Michael G. Witczak, Vice Rector, Professor of Liturgy, St. Francis Seminary, Milwaukee, Wisconsin / Pontifical Liturgical Institute of St. Anselm, Rome, Italy.